SEA FIGHTS
UNDER SAIL

Publishers of the International Library

LIBRAIRIE ERNEST FLAMMARION—France
VERLAG J. F. SCHREIBER—Germany
(in association with Union Verlag, Stuttgart, and Oster, Bundesverlag, Vienna)
WM. COLLINS SONS & CO. LTD.—Great Britain
RIZZOLI EDITORE—Italy
MCGRAW-HILL BOOK COMPANY—United States of America

International Consultants

JEAN-FRANCOIS POUPINEL—France
Ancien Elève Ecole Polytechnique
KLAUS DODERER—Germany
Professor, Frankfurt
MARGARET MEEK—Great Britain
Lecturer in Education at Goldsmiths' College
in the University of London
FAUSTO MARIA BONGIOANNI—Italy
Professor of Education
at the University of Genoa
MARY V. GAVER—United States of America
Professor, Graduate School of Library Science,
Rutgers University

International Editorial Board

HENRI NOGUÈRES
GERHARD SCHREIBER
JAN COLLINS
GIANNI FERRAUTO
HOWARD GRAHAM

CHRISTOPHER LLOYD

SEA FIGHTS UNDER SAIL

COLLINS London and Glasgow

First Edition 1970

ISBN 0 00 100117 5

Printed in the Netherlands by
Smeets Lithographers Weert

CONTENTS

CHAPTER 1

GUNS AND SAILS

The history of sea warfare may be divided into three broad periods: The Age of the Galley, which lasted from antiquity to the battle of Lepanto in 1571, though galleys continued in use for another century in the Mediterranean; the Age of Sail, in which the first great event was the defeat of the Spanish Armada in 1588 and the last was the battle of Navarino in 1827; and the Age of Steam, which continued until the advent of nuclear power. Apart from Lepanto, this book is about some of the great sea fights during the Age of Sail.

How did the sailing ship armed with guns come into existence? It is a long story with which we are not primarily concerned here, but since it was an invention of the greatest importance in European history, it may be as well to describe briefly the nature of its evolution. The significance of the invention may be estimated if we compare medieval Europe, a mass of petty feudal states which made the continent extremely vulnerable to foreign in- vaders, with the continent which later consisted of a few powerful nation states possessing colonies abroad and carrying on an extensive trade with all parts of the world. To a large extent it was this rivalry in maritime trade and empire which caused the growth of navies and the wars in which they were used.

Battle of Navarino

Galleon chasing galley

waters the most famous Long ships were those in which the Vikings conquered large parts of northern Europe. They were shallow, double-ended vessels, which could be beached up rivers. They were easy to handle and were propelled by a square sail on a single mast set amidships. But as trade developed they were found to be useless as cargo carriers, so they ceased to be built after the twelfth century.

The equivalent of the Norse fighting ship in the Mediterranean was the galley, powered by oars and a single lateen or triangular sail. Its distinctive feature was a long, sharp ram, because galley tactics consisted of rowing down upon your enemy, ramming him and boarding his ship. Later on a gun or two was mounted in the bows, but the position of the oars prevented the mounting of guns broadside. With their galley fleets, the city states of Venice, Genoa or Barcelona made themselves into the most important naval powers of that time. The Knights of St John of Malta continued to use galleys in their fights against the Turks right up to the eighteenth century, but the Age of the Galley really ended with the development of the ocean-going ship, which was better armed, stouter in structure, more capacious, and capable of sailing in seas which were too dangerous for the shallow-draft galley.

The technological breakthrough which brought about the change from a Europe which was a mere peninsula of Asia to a Europe which was the centre of the world was the development of the armed, ocean-going sailing-ship. Thereby the limited human power of the oarsmen who manned the galleys was exchanged for the unlimited power of sails, enabling western Europeans to reach and conquer lands across distant seas.

Round ships and long ships

In the Middle Ages there was a distinction between the Round ship used for trading purposes and the Long ship used for war. In northern

Venetian galleys of the largest size—over 600 tons and 100 feet long—were often used for trading purposes. A squadron of these used to visit Southampton and Antwerp every year until 1536, when it became obvious that the future lay with the galleon, as the Round ship came to be called. Originally the Venetians called a large galley a *galeone;* or if she had masts as well as oars, a *galeasse*—a powerful transitional type of warship. The true galleon, as developed by the Spanish and the English, was a four masted ship, square rigged on the fore and main masts, lateen rigged on the mizzen and bonaventure mizzen masts, with a low beak-head like a galley's ram instead of the high over-hanging superstructure of her predecessor, the Great Ship or Nef (Latin: *navis*).

The galleon ruled the seas in the sixteenth century when it had developed from the broad, almost round cargo vessel of earlier times. Early ships were steered by a steering oar on one side (hence the word "starboard" or right-hand side, as contrasted with "larboard" or "port", the side nearest the quay when a ship was loaded through a porthole). No one knows who invented the rudder built into the stern to replace the steering oar, but a seal of Bergen in the thirteenth century suggests that it was a northern invention. Rudders were worked by horizontal bars called tillers until the steering wheel was introduced about 1700.

Soldiers at sea

When a privately-owned cargo ship was used for war, "castles" were erected at bow and stern to give the defenders the advantage of height. From these, missiles of all sorts could be hurled down upon the enemy—arrows, spears, rocks, boiling oil, or Greek Fire, an incendiary mixture of naphtha, bitumen, resin and oil, to which sulphur and saltpetre (the principal ingredients of gunpowder) were later added. Until guns increased the range of action, thereby altering the whole pattern of warfare, it was a matter of fighting a land battle by sea. Broadswords, not broadsides, decided the issue. Soldiers did most

of the fighting, leaving the mariners to manage the sails, hence the word "sailor". In what the chronicler, Froissart, called the very murderous and bloody fights during the Hundred Years' War, huddled groups of ships came to close quarters without any thought of tactics or battle formation.

"Castles" became integral parts of the ship. In English the word "forecastle" (pronounced "fo'c'stle") remains, but the "aftercastle" was later called "poop" (Latin: *puppis*). A single mast was the rule until the fifteenth century, when two, three and later four masts appear in bigger ships. Early galleons maintained the castle tradition by being built up high at bow and stern, with a low waist between. The new type of galleon developed by the English diminished the height of these superstructures, which made ships difficult to handle because of wind resistance. When more guns were mounted broadside, this new type of galleon, of which Drake's *Revenge* during the Armada campaign is a good example, became a powerful, fast and manoeuvrable means of waging war.

Galleon Griffin *in 1588*

The advent of the gun

Guns had been known from early in the fourteenth century, soon after which the poet Petrarch was complaining of "those instruments which discharge balls of metal with the most tremendous noise and flashes of fire." They were almost as dangerous to those who used them as they were to the enemy, because they were built up from bars of iron welded into crude tubes which were strengthened by hoops. They were loaded at the breach. About the year 1500 smaller guns were being cast in a single piece in iron, brass or bronze. These were muzzle-loaders, a cartridge of gunpowder behind the ball being touched off with a match of smouldering twine through a small hole in the rear of the barrel. The day of the breach-loader type of gun did not return until after the age of sail was over.

Medieval cannon were too heavy for ships, though small guns capable of killing men but not injuring ships were put on board. The *Christopher of the Tower* (i.e. a royal ship) of 1406 is said to be the first warship to be thus armed. Heavier guns could not be mounted because of the danger of straining the timbers until a shipwright named Descharges of Brest began to cut holes in the side of a ship in 1501. A line of such gunports is found in the French ship *Louise* of about that date, and in the *Henri Grace à Dieu* or *Great Harry* of 1514. She was the first English battleship, mounting forty-four muzzle-loaders and 122 small breach-loaders. Her example was followed by the Swedes, who (after the Germans) became the best gunfounders in Europe.

The Great Harry *of 1514*

The Navy grows up

In this way the gunned warship came into existence, Henry VIII of England possessing the largest navy of his day, together with dockyards and an administrative system consisting of the Admiralty and the Navy Board. The ocean routes were being opened by the Portuguese and the Spanish who used, at first, the caravel, which was not a warship, or the much larger carrack for the long route to India. Though not intended for war, these huge ships carried a formidable armament because the seas swarmed with pirates and enemies of all kinds.

By the end of the century the English and the Dutch had so improved the galleon that she was more than a match for these big ships. Just as the English fought the Spaniards in the West Indies, so the Dutch fought the Portuguese in the Indian Ocean. A Jesuit priest wrote early in the seventeenth century that "the Portuguese galleons are noteworthy because of their great size and their many facilities. Each one looks like a castle and is furnished with eighty or more bronze guns. The deck is so spacious that the sailors often play ball. . . . These vessels would be unequalled if they were not such sluggish movers and could be better manned. The Dutch vessels, which are handier to manœuvre by the wind, overcome the Portuguese galleons very easily."

Compass, chart and chronometer

The great contribution made by the Portuguese was in the art of navigation. From the days of Prince Henry the Navigator, her explorers in their caravels were using not only the compass (first mentioned at Amalfi in 1187) but the cross-staff,

which developed into the sextant, in order to establish their latitude by measuring the elevation of the sun at noon. It took another three centuries before the longitude could be accurately estimated. The Portuguese and the Catalans from Barcelona and Majorca were also producing beautiful and comparatively accurate marine charts. With such advances in oceanic navigation, ships no longer needed to follow a known coastline. They could stretch out with confidence beyond the horizon in sturdy, well-armed and well-rigged ships, even if they did not always know exactly where they were.

After the great strides taken in shipbuilding, gunnery and navigation during the period 1450-1550, progress slowed down because something like the optimum had been reached in the size of ships and in the range of their guns. Of course, improvements were made during the next two centuries, which will be mentioned in due course, but technological progress was incredibly slow compared with modern times. Thus the range of artillery, a little over a

Use of the cross-staff

Use of the astrolabe

ORBIS LONGITVDINES REPERTÆ E MAGNETIS A POLO DECLINATIONE.
Magnete paulum vtrinque sæpe deuia   Dat inuenire portum vbique Plancius.

Obtaining a longitude by using a compass and an astrolabe

11

mile, had hardly increased between the Armada and the battle of Trafalgar, though new short range guns such as the carronade of 1779 were invented and they were aimed better and fired more safely by means of a flint lock. But a captain of a warship still had to manœuvre his whole ship to bring a broadside to bear, rather than alter the position of the gun itself. Other notable advances were the Dutch improvements in rigging, the French scientific design of ships, and the English use of copper sheathing on the bottom to check the damage done by the naval worm, *teredo navalis*. The greatest improvement to the safety of ships was the solution of the old problem of longitude by the invention of the chronometer, which was first demonstrated on the voyages of Captain James Cook.

The gun-deck of the Vasa today

Ships of war

Such things affected all ships. What we are concerned with in this book is the warship, which could not be clearly distinguished from the merchant ship until the middle of the seventeenth century. Only then was it obvious that a ship could not be designed to carry many guns as well as cargo. Towards the beginning of that century the English built the *Sovereign of the Seas* (1637), the first three-decker with three masts and 100 guns, the prototype of the first rate line-of-battle ship. She was of 1,637 tons, a more powerful ship than the Swedish *Vasa* of 1,400 tons, which sank on her maiden voyage in 1628. She, too, was a three-decker, though she only carried 64 guns when she sank. By a miracle of salvage, she has now been recovered

from the mud of Stockholm harbour and is to-day the oldest survival from the age of sail. Neither the *Sovereign,* nor the *Vasa* differ basically in design from the *Victory* (2,162 tons), which was on active service from 1765 to 1815 and remained in the water until 1924, when she was restored to her present state in dry dock at Portsmouth. The third surviving sailing warship is the single-decked U.S. frigate *Constitution* ("Old Ironsides" of 2,200 tons), built in 1797 and now at Boston.

The tactical revolution necessitated by the mounting of guns broadside was at last complete. As we have seen, in the days of galleys when the object was to ram the enemy, a line abreast formation was the rule. Now it became line ahead, so that the maximum use could be made of the guns mounted broadside. Tactical instructions and signals began to evolve from about 1650 in order to control the vast fleets which fought in the Anglo-Dutch and Anglo-French wars. The ideal was for each fleet to fire broadsides at each other as they passed in line ahead formation on opposite tacks. As we shall see, there were innumerable mischances, such as a sudden shift in the wind, which spoiled such model battles. But the broad distinction between line-of-battle ships, that is to say ships of two or three decks of guns which were strong enough to lie in the line of battle, and single-decked smaller ships, such as frigates, sloops and brigs, had come to stay.

If an admiral occupied the windward position with his line of battle, it gave him the chance to show some tactical initiative; moreover, because the thick smoke from his guns drifted down upon the enemy, he enjoyed better visibility. On the other hand, some fleets, especially

Title page of the first maritime atlas, 1588

the French, preferred the leeward position, because they could fire their guns on the up roll of the ship to damage masts and rigging and then bear away before the wind to break off action. Since it was impossible to sink a wooden ship with solid shot, most ships were destroyed by fire or by being forced on the rocks. As will be seen, fleet tactics reached such a peak of perfection that a decisive victory at sea became almost impossible until new methods of signalling enabled an admiral like Nelson to be more flexible in the way he handled his line of battle.

By the time of the last generation who fought under sail the experience of three centuries of sea warfare left little to be developed in the art of seamanship, or in the building of warships under sail. The navies of the world awaited the next technical revolution, that of iron and steam.

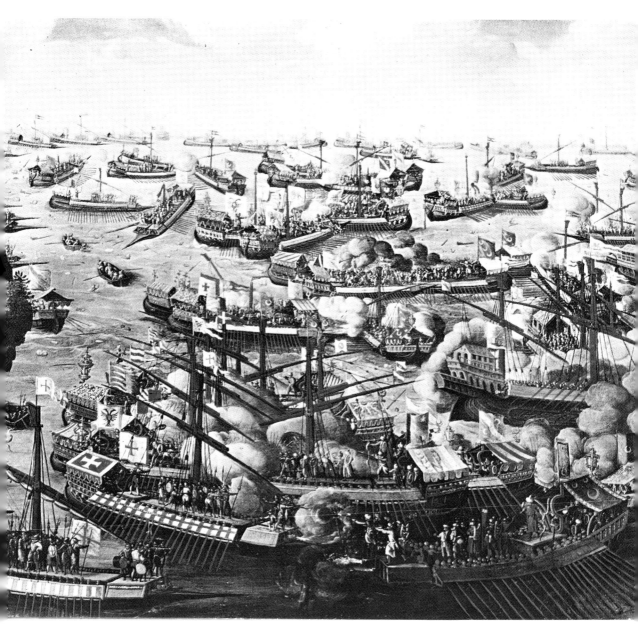

14

CHAPTER 2

LEPANTO

When the Ottoman Turks captured Constantinople in 1453, Cardinal Bessarion told the Doge of Venice that "it was a terrible thing to relate and to be deplored by all who have in them any spark of humanity, and especially by Christians. Much danger threatens Italy, not to mention other lands, if the violent assaults of the most ferocious barbarians are not checked."

Both horns of the Muslim crescent threatened Europe, one pointing towards Vienna, the other towards Spain, because all the southern shores of the Mediterranean were controlled by the Sultan, who could call upon the notorious Barbary corsairs of Algiers and Tunis to assist his own formidable armies with their ships. The Turks themselves were not a sea-going people, though they managed to clear the Genoese out of the Black Sea and begin a long series of wars against the Republic of Venice by conquering its possessions in the Eastern Mediterranean, such as Cyprus, Crete and Greek towns like Lepanto (the name given by the Venetians to their settlement at the western end of the Gulf of Corinth, now called Naupaktos).

The famous corsairs were of Moorish rather than Turkish stock, but as Muslims they were equally committed to the conquest of Christendom, especially after

Battle of Lepanto— the two flagships engaged

Ferdinand and Isabella had expelled them from southern Spain, thereby blunting the western horn of the Muslim crescent. Based on Algiers, the red-bearded brothers, known as the Barbarossas by Europeans— Uruz and Kheyr-ed-din—were attacking Christian shipping in the western Mediterranean at the same time as the Ottoman Turks were advancing in the eastern part. Kheyr-ed-din, the rival of the famous Genoese admiral Andrea Doria, is described as being "portly and majestic; well-proportioned and robust; very hairy with a beard extremely bushy; before his hair turned grey and hoary, it was bright auburn." He defeated Doria at the great sea battle of Previsa (known to the ancients as Actium) in 1538, when in alliance with the Ottoman Porte. The Sultan persuaded him to expand and reorganize the Turkish navy, so that before his death in 1546 it was as powerful as that of any European nation. For many years no Turkish ship left the Golden Horn without saluting the memory of the greatest of Mediterranean pirates and the founder of Turkish sea power. It was his successor, Ochiali, Pasha of Algiers, the last of the great corsairs, who proved the outstanding admiral at the battle of Lepanto.

A galleon of 1565, by Bruegel

The formation of the Holy League

When the Knights of St John were driven out of Rhodes by the advancing Turks, they settled at Malta which, in its turn, was beseiged in 1565. Their heroic defence of the island was the first set-back to Turkish forces, which were threatening to overrun the crumbling Venetian empire. The Balkans had been conquered by Suleiman the Magnificent, who died at the head of his army in Hungary. He was succeeded by the feeble Selim (known as "the Sot" on account of his addiction to drink), but the Grand Vizier, the generals and the Capitan Pasha at the head of the fleet were able men, who continued the advance of Islam at the expense of Venice. Realizing the magnitude of the threat to European civilization, and animated by the heroic defence of Malta by the Knights of St John, the Pope, Pius V, called on His Most Christian Majesty, Philip II of Spain, for help in forming a Holy League in 1571 to embark on a counter-attack which

Don John of Austria

may be considered as the last crusade against the forces of Islam.

Only a few days before the battle of Lepanto was fought, the news reached the fleet that Famagusta, the last fortress in Cyprus, had fallen. The story of the accompanying atrocities (the skin of the Venetian governor was stuffed with straw and sent to the Sultan) sharpened the swords of the representatives of European chivalry who were determined on revenge.

The Holy League was formed only when the Turks threatened to advance up the Adriatic. It was an unstable alliance between ancient rivals which could only be held together by a common fear of invasion and by good leadership on the part of the commander-in-chief. The forces gathering at Messina in Sicily were very large, but they were provided by states which did not trust each others' motives—Malta, Venice, Genoa, Spain, the Papacy and Naples, together with German troops sent by the Holy Roman Emperor. To weld this cosmopolitan fleet into anything like a unified force demanded high qualities of leadership and tact; yet the man put in supreme command—Don John of Austria—was only twenty-four years old.

The young commander-in-chief

He was the illegitimate son of the Emperor Charles V, and so the brother of Philip II of Spain, whose navy he commanded, though he was a soldier by profession. He is described as "a youth of an active and well-developed frame, with light hair and a countenance very pleasing and comely." He was born in Bavaria and had seen service in Spain, but not naval service. For this reason, older men were ap-

Miguel de Cervantes

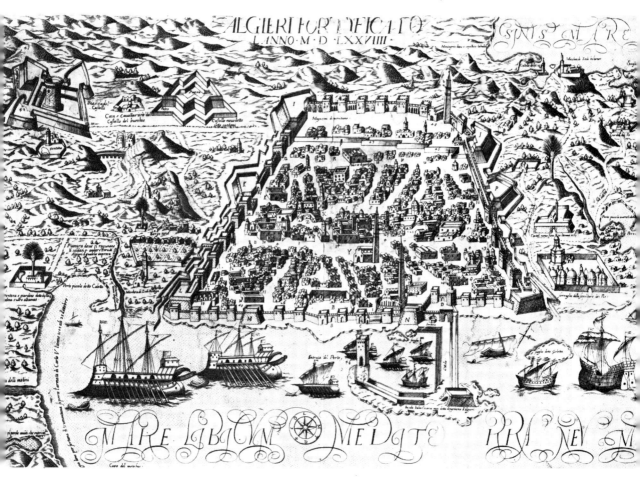

Algiers, the home of the Barbary corsair

pointed to advise him on the tactics of galley warfare—Sebastiano Veniero, aged seventy-five, soon to become Doge of Venice; Prince Antonio Colonna, who commanded the Papal galleys; the Marquis of Santa Cruz, commanding the Spanish reserve, whom Cervantes calls "a thunderbolt of war and a father to his soldiers, a brave and invincible captain."

For us today, the most famous man in the fleet, though now no more than a humble soldier, was Miguel de Cervantes, who was the same age as Don John. His left hand was shattered by a shot during the battle. As he proudly wrote many years later, it was "a wound which, although it appears ugly, he holds for lovely, because he received it on the most memorable and lofty occasion that past centuries have beheld." It was he who laughed Europe out of the age of chivalry by writing *Don Quixote* thirty years later.

The Age of the Galley also ended at Lepanto. Most of the vessels on both sides were large examples of this type, 100–150 feet long, rowed by twenty-six pairs of oars, which were themselves ten feet long, so that each was manned by four galley slaves, convicts or prisoners. On the Ottoman side, the Capitan Pasha, or commander-in-chief, was noted for his humanity towards these miserable creatures, nearly all of them Christian prisoners. "Friends," he told them in Spanish, "I expect you to do your duty to me this day, in return for what I have done for you. If I win the battle, I promise you your liberty; if the day is yours, Allah has given it to you."

The fact that the galley was declining as a weapon of war is shown by Don John's order that in each vessel the ten-foot beakhead should be removed, so that more reliance might be put on the guns in the bows, the largest of which fired a 40 pound shot. The Venetians also contributed six huge *galeasses,* powered by both oars and sails, armed with sixty guns firing a still larger ball. There were a good many genuine sailing vessels in the fleet called *fregata* (frigates), but they played no part in the battle, being used as fast despatch boats or scouts: they had nothing in common with the later single-decked warships also called frigates. The oared galley which fought at the battle of Lepanto was still a vessel dependent on rowers, soldiers and officers, who used the gangway which ran the length of the ship over the heads of the oarsmen, and who manned the few guns at bow or stern.

The fleet which gathered at Messina under the command of Don John was the largest ever seen in the Mediterranean, being composed of about 26,000 Italians, Germans and Spaniards (apart from the oarsmen) on board 300 vessels of all sorts—galleys, *galeasses* and frigates. When the news arrived that the Ottoman fleet had been sighted near Corfu, Don John moved across the Adriatic towards Greece. Action was joined on 7th October, 1571, in the Bay of Lepanto at the mouth of the Gulf of Patras leading to Corinth.

The Turkish commanders

In command of the Turkish fleet was Ali Pasha, with ninety-six galleys in the centre division. On his right, nearest the land, was Mohammed Sirocco with fifty-six galleys from Egypt. On his left were ninety-three Algerine galleys under

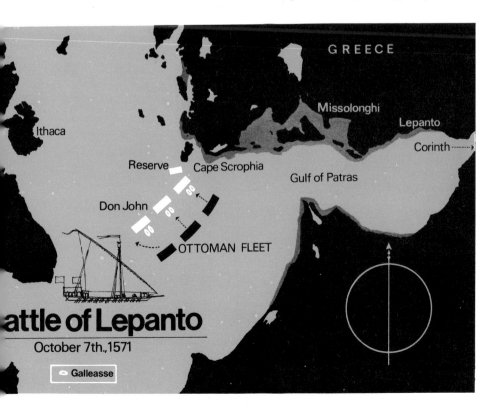

GREECE

Ithaca

Missolonghi

Lepanto

Corinth ------>

Reserve Cape Scrophia

Gulf of Patras

Don John

OTTOMAN FLEET

attle of Lepanto
October 7th., 1571

Galleasse

Fresco of the Battle of Lepanto from the Doge's Palace, Venice

the ablest admiral present. He was called by the Christians Uluch Ali, or Ochiala, a westernized form of Ali-el-Uluji, meaning Ali the Renegade, because he was born in Calabria and had been captured by the Barbary corsairs as a child. Now he was Pasha of Algiers. According to Cervantes, he was "a worthy man morally, and he treated his slaves with great humanity"— perhaps because, having been one himself, he knew their sufferings. He was certainly a first-rate seaman

and he nearly won the battle by his tactics.

Ali Pasha commanded a force little inferior to that of Don John—some 250 galleys and 25,000 soldiers, the best fighters being the Janissaries, who were the *corps d'élite* of the Ottoman army. Like Uluch Ali, they were of Christian birth but had been taken away from their parents at an early age in order to be trained as professional soldiers forming what might be called an imperial guard.

A new tactic

The traditional lines of battle for galley tactics, that is to say in line abreast, were formed on both sides, covering nearly two miles in length. But Don John made an important innovation by placing at the head of each division two *galeasses,* whose fire power broke the force of the Turkish attack as their galleys rowed down to join battle. On the landward side he placed sixty-three Venetian galleys under Agostino Barbarigo; in the centre was his own flagship flanked by Veniero and Colonna with another sixty-three; on the right to seaward was a mixed force of the same size under Doria of Genoa; in reserve was Santa Cruz with thirty-five Spanish galleys. All flagships flew red pennons to distinguish them from the Turkish ships which flew green flags from their mastheads. Colonna displayed the Papal banner, Veniero the Lion of St Mark, and Don John himself the sanctified standard of the Holy League.

"Signor," he said to old Veniero as he surveyed the long Ottoman line, "you must put forth all your claws, for it will be a hard fight." The Turks were seasoned warriors, with a long series of victories behind them. The young commander-in-chief knew how fragile was the alliance he commanded and how easy it would be for any part of his force to desert.

Battle is joined

The battle began early on a sunny October day with the Turkish right wing advancing in line abreast, their oars beating the water like the wings of huge sea birds. Sirocco was trying to outflank Barbarigo by getting between him and the shore. The latter was wounded in the eye by an arrow; but before Sirocco had achieved his aim he himself was knocked overboard and then retrieved from the water by a Venetian, who promptly cut off his head.

In the centre, the Turkish onslaught was checked by the heavy fire of the *galeasses.* The enemy had never experienced the use of artillery on this scale before. Heavy shot suddenly hurtled among them, smashing oars, maiming the rowers on the benches, killing the soldiers on deck. The impact of their onset was broken, but scores of galleys rowed past to crash their iron-plated rams into Don John's ships and throw grappling irons on board. The centre soon became a mêlée of whirling scimitars, stabbing swords and blazing arquebuses. The two flagships steered for each other. When, eventually, they came to grips, it was Don John's arquebusiers who finally carried the day. In spite of wearing a talisman made from the tooth of the Prophet, Ali Pasha was shot and one of the boarders cut off his head and stuck it on a pike. After that there was little resistance.

Meanwhile, on their right, things were not going so well for the Christians. The wily Uluch pretended that he was going to outflank Doria, thereby drawing him away from the centre in order to parry the threat. As soon as a wide gap had been made, the Algerines suddenly reversed course in order to steer through and attack Don John from the side. When Santa Cruz saw what was intended he promptly moved up the reserve to block the gap. Panic broke out when it was seen that the Capitan Pasha's galley had been captured and Uluch made good his retreat. Scores of galleys were left to be sunk or wrecked: 113 were burned on the spot, and 117 prizes were towed back to Messina, their standards trailing ignominiously in the water.

No one knows exactly the number of casualties, but it is probable that they were higher than in any other battle at sea because of the boarding and hand to hand fighting which took place. One estimate of the Turkish figure is higher than the total force engaged, but it is known that over 8,000 prisoners were taken. On the Christian side, about that number were killed and twice as many wounded. Seventeen galley captains among the Venetians were killed that day, and sixty Knights of St John met a crusader's death. The Venetians felt bitter about their losses because the Genoese got off so lightly. Doria was accused of treachery and cowardice, but the truth was simply that he had been outmanœuvred by Uluch Ali. Doria alone of the commanders ·was blamed for his conduct: all the others returned in triumph to their respective cities.

A Christian victory

For the first time in history the standard of the Prophet had been captured by Christians. The moral effect of the victory was very great, because it destroyed the legend of Ottoman invincibility. Venice breathed again and splendid frescoes were painted on the walls of the Doge's palace to commemorate the event. Nevertheless, as the Sultan said, "They have cut off my beard, but it will grow again." The battle of Lepanto did not finally break the Turkish advance: it diverted the invaders from the sea to the land, until over a hundred years later the Ottoman forces were defeated by Prince Eugene outside Vienna and the tide at last receded.

Don John died of a fever seven years after his victory, when he was in command of the Spanish army in the Low Countries, vainly attempting to suppress the rebellion of the Dutch. A few months before his death, Sir Francis Walsingham, the English Secretary of State, met him while trying to negotiate a peace settlement. He told Queen Elizabeth: "Surely I never saw a gentleman for personage, speech, wit and entertainment comparable to him. If pride do not overthrow him, he is like to become a great personage." He was certainly a great leader of men, and when he died he was only thirty-one years old.

Andrea Doria

CHAPTER 3

THE SPANISH ARMADA

The ocean routes of the world were opened by the Portuguese and Spanish explorers of one astonishing generation. Between 1467, when Bartholomew Diaz discovered the Cape of Good Hope, and 1522, when the *Vitoria* returned home after the first circumnavigation of the globe (her captain, Ferdinand Magellan, having been killed during the course of the voyage), the foundations of new maritime empires in the east and in the west were laid. When, in 1580, the crowns of Portugal and Spain were united in the person of Philip II, the riches which flowed from the Spanish conquests in America and from the Portuguese control of the spice trade from the east naturally excited the jealousy of the less favoured nations of western Europe.

What the English in particular objected to was the Spanish claim to control not only their vast colonial territories which were sparsely inhabited, but the seas surrounding them. Hitherto these claims had been unchallenged, because the English and the French were embroiled in the Reformation and the Dutch had not yet made themselves independent of Spanish rule. When it became clear that the Spanish possessions overseas were virtually undefended by a maritime force, adventurous seamen began to penetrate the Caribbean and

A tapestry of Armada ships

Sir John Hawkins

cross the Isthmus of Panama. Since the discovery of a North-West Passage to the riches of Asia now seemed impossible, there were many who were attracted by the chance of easy loot to be won on the coasts of Central America, generally known as the Spanish Main. The most important of these early adventurers was John Hawkins of Plymouth, who was to become Treasurer of the Navy. His third voyage ended in disaster at San Juan de Ulua in 1568, when a ship which he had hired from the queen to transport slaves from Africa was captured by a Spanish force. He claimed that he was engaged on legitimate trade and that he had been treacherously attacked. The Spanish authorities took a different view. Though Hawkins and his young cousin. Francis Drake, escaped, as far as they were concerned a lifelong conflict with Spain had begun.

Drake, the Great Captain

In this private war (for Queen Elizabeth had as yet no desire to break with Spain), two of the strongest motives were a lust for gold and a crusade on the part of Protestant adventurers against the iniquities of the Spanish Inquisition. Drake personified such motives to a remarkable degree. It was he who made his name by daring raids on what he called "the treasure house of the world", and it was his less successful friends who were captured and put to death by the Inquisition. His voyage round the world during the years 1577-80 was the climax of those years of private warfare. It was also the event which heralded the appearance of a new sea power which would challenge the supremacy of Spain. Not only was his voyage astonishingly suc-

Sir Francis Drake,
wearing the jewel
presented to him by
Queen Elizabeth

cessful in the prizes which he took, but he was the first sea captain to bring his own ship home.

It is not easy to define Drake's status at that time. The Spaniards, of course, called him a *corsario* or pirate. He regarded himself as a privateer, sailing with the approval of the queen and her ministers. He was certainly not what we should call a naval officer. The Elizabethan age was the golden age of privateering, that is to say a form of warfare in which privately owned vessels cruised with the consent of the queen against her enemies. Privateers were subject to the law of prize, so that a proportion of any profits made by the capture of ships or cargoes was handed over to the government. The queen invested heavily in Drake's voyage and she knighted him on board the *Golden Hind* when he returned after making a profit of forty-seven pounds on every pound invested.

Privateers or pirates?

Privateering remained a legitimate form of warfare as long as the age of sail lasted. But it was lawful only after war had been declared and after the owner of such a ship had been given a letter of marque as a sign of his government's approval; otherwise he might be regarded as a pirate and hanged as a criminal. In the history of all navies, privateering is an essential preliminary to the great fleet actions of later times, because the number of ships owned by the state is small at that stage and there are plenty of adventurers who prefer to cruise on their own account, unfettered by government orders or codes of professional conduct. Sometimes, when they have made their names by their own efforts, they are employed by the state as officers. Such was the career of men

Howard of Effingham, the Lord Admiral

like Francis Drake in England, Jean Bart in France and Paul Jones in America. The regular naval officer emerges from the privateer only when a naval tradition has been formed and a career has been opened for him. In Elizabethan times, the royal navy was a small affair, but the number of seamen willing to cruise upon the Spanish Main, or attempt to intercept the treasure fleets from Peru and the carracks from the East Indies was enormous.

Convoys for defence

It took some time for Spain to realize that such men offered a serious challenge to seaborne trade and the security of her colonies in the West Indies. Gradually her defences were improved and her treasure fleets guarded by heavily armed escorts, so that it was the Spanish who invented the convoy system. Thus, the early career of Drake was much more successful. In 1585 he was able to capture towns like San Domingo in Hispaniola and St Augustine in Florida in a series of brilliant amphibious operations which mark the beginning of the open war with Spain. Ten years later he died off Porto Bello. In between lay his greatest triumph in the defeat of the Spanish Armada.

England learns her lessons

Spain was also slow to realize that a new epoch in naval warfare had begun. Her stately galleons still retained the high "castles" of earlier times, and her ships were largely manned by soldiers. But by now the gun had made hand-to-hand fighting out of date. Long after it had been proved to the contrary, an Italian writer, still thinking in terms of galley warfare, insisted that "to hit the enemy at a long distance with artillery cannot be the purpose of a navy." The English, on the other hand, after twenty years of war with Spain, rightly claimed that "experience teaches how sea fights in these days come seldom to boarding, but are chiefly performed by the great artillery breaking down masts, yards; tearing, raking and bilging ships."

Not, it will be noticed, in sinking them. The solid iron shot fired by the guns of even the most powerful ships could only knock holes in the sides of stoutly built galleons. Nevertheless, ships so damaged were liable to be wrecked, and there was always the danger of fire on board, on account of the amount of loose gunpowder lying about the decks in an action. It was well said in those days that fire was more feared than water.

The armament which warships carried on one or two decks consisted of cannon firing a thirty pound ball, the eighteen pound culverin, the nine pound demi-culverin, and a host of smaller upper deck weapons variously called sakers, serpentines, murderers etc. In the English fleet which fought the Armada, 84% of the guns were of the demi-culverin type, because the recoil of heavier guns strained the timbers of the ships. A well-armed galleon of the newer type, such as Drake's flagship, the *Revenge,* a 450-ton ship, 92 feet long with a beam of 32 feet, mounted thirty-four guns. The *Ark Royal* of 800 tons mounted forty-four, whereas the older and larger *Triumph* of 1,100 tons had only forty-two.

When comparing Spanish ships with English in 1588 the former certainly looked larger because of their high poops and forecastles. In close combat they would have

been very formidable on account of the number of small guns which they carried. On the other hand, the lower, faster English ships which they called "race built" galleons were more manœuvrable and more heavily armed. In tonnage there was not much to choose: the largest Spanish galleon was of 1,250 tons, mounting only thirty small guns; the largest English ship was the *Triumph* of 1,100 tons, with forty-two guns. Only fourteen Spanish ships were over 800 tons. Nor did the fleets differ much in numbers: the Armada was composed of 130 ships all told, the English fleet at Plymouth numbered 102, with fifty more in reserve in the Thames. It is significant that only sixteen of the sixty-nine galleons were owned by the queen: all the rest were armed merchantmen, of which there were only forty-one in the Spanish fleet.

As in so many other ways, Elizabeth got her subjects to do what in modern times would be done by the state, and she had plenty of privateers to call on.

Rival sea powers

The reasons for the sailing of the Invincible Armada, (the word armada means armed fleet) as the Spaniards called this armed fleet, were manifold. As we have seen, for ten years past Spanish possessions in America had been harassed by the English and now Drake threatened her communications across the Atlantic. Elizabeth was also openly assisting the Dutch rebels who were fighting for independence against the Duke of Parma in the Low Countries. By way of reprisal, the King of Spain seized all English shipping in Spanish ports

The Ark Royal, *the English flagship*

King Philip II of Spain

population, the best army and the greatest wealth of any nation in the world. No wonder the scanty population of England and Wales (Scotland was a separate kingdom and Ireland was hardly colonized) stood in awe of Spanish power, or that Elizabeth postponed the inevitable conflict as long as she could.

The Armada, otherwise known as the "Enterprise against England," was planned two years before it sailed. Originally the Marquis of Santa Cruz, who had fought at Lepanto and knew that an era in which the gun predominated had dawned, was to have commanded it. When he died, his views were transmitted to his successor, who was warned not to try gun duels with the English because it was known that their artillery was superior. This successor was the Duke of Medina Sidonia, a great nobleman but without experience of sea fighting. The same might be said of Lord Howard of Effingham, the Lord Admiral of the English fleet at Plymouth, though he accepted the appointment more willingly. The point was that only a great nobleman could control such a variety of unruly subordinates. In Howard's case it was just as important to stop Drake firing on Frobisher, whom he detested, as to defeat the Spaniards.

When it was obvious that the Armada was preparing to sail for the invasion of England, Drake was allowed to carry out a brilliant surprise attack on the ships in Cadiz harbour in 1587, an operation known as "the singeing of the King of Spain's beard". But the squadrons from the Mediterranean provinces of Spain had not yet reached the fleet, so that all that was achieved by the raid was the postponement for a year of the sailing of the main body.

and became deeply implicated in plots to replace the Protestant Elizabeth with the Catholic Mary, Queen of Scots. After her execution, the religious complexion of what was now open, even if still undeclared, war became more marked and the Pope blessed the banners of the Armada when it sailed from Lisbon on May 30th, 1588.

Philip was not only King of Spain and Portugal and the Two Sicilies (Naples and Sicily), but Lord of the Indies and the ruler of what is now Belgium and Holland. His country possessed the largest

The Armada sails

The majority of the 27,000 men who ultimately sailed from Lisbon were soldiers, who despised the seamen. Furthermore, many of the Spanish ships were unarmed transports for horses and supplies, because the object was to reach Parma's army of 17,000 men in the Low Countries and then cross the Channel to enter the Thames. Four galleys sailed from Lisbon, but they were forced to leave the fleet after encountering a gale in the Bay of Biscay. Two huge *galeasses* also sailed to protect the *San Martin* flagship. But what really saved the Armada on the first stage of its voyage (since Sidonia reached Calais with the loss of only two ships) was the tight military formation which it maintained. The English described this as a crescent or half moon, but they saw it from astern. In reality it was shaped like an eagle, with the flagship as the head, warship squadrons from Castile and Portugal on either wing, the transports and merchantmen as the body, and protective squadrons forming the tail. The fleet must have looked most impressive in this formation, with the towering superstructures of the galleons painted in brilliant colours and carved in gold, the sails emblazoned with pictures of the saints or decorative coats of arms, every mast trailing long coloured pennons.

The weakest points about the Armada were bad victualling, inadequate water supplies for a long voyage, and the unhygienic conditions in which the men lived. They had hardly left Lisbon when a gale struck them, forcing Sidonia to put into Corunna, where he begged the king to abandon the whole plan. Philip refused, so the Armada continued on its way under a despondent commander. Another gale in the Bay of Biscay drove the galleys back

Track of the Armada around the British Isles

31

FORBISHERUS ouans NEPTUNIA regna frequentat
Pre patria at tandem glande peremptus obit

Sir Martin Frobisher

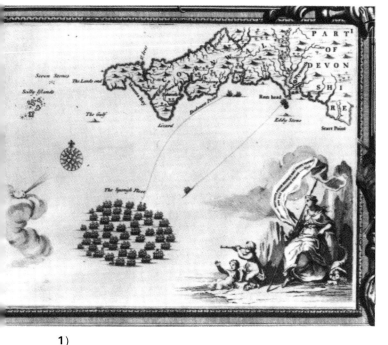

1)

and flew back under press of sail to Plymouth. Here had been gathered since May, the main body of the English fleet of 102 ships under Lord Howard of Effingham, with three experienced vice-admirals under him—Sir Francis Drake, Sir John Hawkins, and Sir Martin Frobisher. Most of their men were seasoned privateers, though there were also volunteers and conscripted men. A reserve of fifty ships under Lord Henry Seymour lay in the Thames. On shore, regiments were formed (Sir Walter Raleigh commanding in the west), beacons were built on hilltops to be fired as signals when the enemy was in sight, and all the church bells were ordered to be rung. The best troops were encamped at Tilbury on the Thames, where they were inspired by speeches by the queen herself: "I know I have the body of a weak and feeble woman, but I have the heart and stomach of a king, and of the king of England too, and I think foul scorn that Parma or Spain, or any prince of Europe, should dare to invade the borders of my realm."

The Armada enters the Channel

The Armada entered the Channel on July 19th, according to the old English calendar, July 31st, according to the modern Spanish one. Tradition says that the news reached Howard and Drake as they were playing bowls on Plymouth Hoe. It is likely enough; but the story that Drake said, "There's time to finish the game and beat the Spaniards too," does not appear until two hundred years later. There was certainly no time to be lost in putting to sea. The fleet was embayed, with the wind blowing directly into Plymouth Sound. It was only by consummate seaman-

to port. Nevertheless, the fleet reformed when it reached the Cornish coast and began its week-long majestic progress up Channel.

Captain Fleming, one of the scouts sent out to give warning of the enemy's approach, saw this vast concourse of shipping off the Lizard

ship that the ships were got to sea to take up a position astern of the Spanish fleet. If Sidonia had not so strictly adhered to his orders to join Parma, he might have destroyed the English at Plymouth just as Drake had done at Cadiz the previous year.

For the whole of the next week the English warily kept their distance, snapping up any ship that fell behind, steadily continuing their harassing pursuit, but never daring to close. On the first night, Drake was told to lead the fleet with a lantern at his topmast. Suddenly it disappeared. He rejoined the next morning with the excuse that he had turned aside to investigate some strange sail (they were Baltic traders) and found the great galleon *Nuestra Señora del Rosario* disabled after a collision. He had taken possession of her and sent her to Dartmouth. She and the *San Salvador,* sent into Weymouth, were the only two big ships captured from the Armada.

On Sunday afternoon, August 6th, the Armada wearily reached Calais. Parma was not ready and there was nowhere to anchor in safety. At this point the Dutch Sea Beggars come into the story. They were the naval element of the Dutch fighting for independence. Based on Flushing, their flyboats, under the command of Justin of Nassau, controlled the mouth of the Scheldt. The main Spanish army was at Antwerp, where hundreds of invasion barges were being built, but they could not get out. With the English harrying them out at sea, the Dutch preventing the army from sailing, the shallow water along the coast from Calais to Gravelines and Dunkirk studded with sandbanks, the small harbour at Calais offering no security, the Invincible Armada was now in a most dangerous situation.

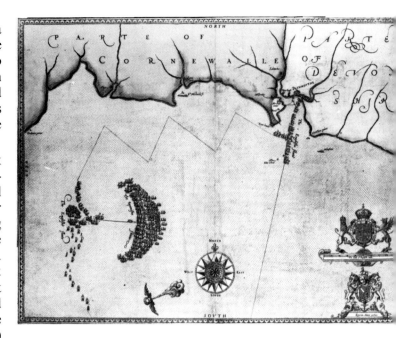

2)

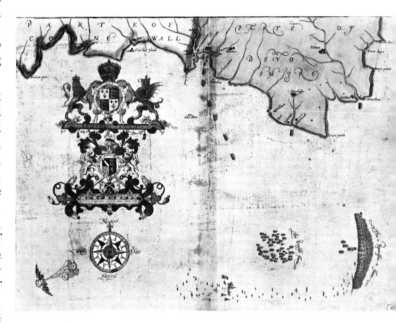

3)

Three contemporary charts by Ryther of the progress of the Armada
1) off the Lizard
2) off Plymouth
3) off Start Point

Fire-ships and a lee shore

Fireships launched against the Armada off Calais

It was Drake who suggested how to take advantage of the opportunity provided by a wind blowing directly on shore. Fire-ships were prepared from the smaller vessels which had now joined the fleet. Barrels of tar and stacks of faggots piled on their decks made them combustible. Then, when night fell, with wind and tide in their favour, they were loosed upon the Spanish galleons as they lay at anchor. Fire-ships were far more dangerous than gunfire to ships huddled together without room to manœuvre. The galleons farther out cut their anchor cables to escape and drifted blindly along the coast in the darkness. Those caught in harbour were burned or run on shore and wrecked.

At sunrise on Monday morning the Armada lay scattered along the coast eastward towards Gravelines. A Spanish friar says that hardly a man slept that night: "We went along all wondering when we should strike one of those sandbanks." Now was the chance to batter the enemy with gunfire and force them against the land. Drake led the "first charge", as he called it, for the English were in no sort of order. Each ship in turn bore down before the wind to deliver a broadside and then turned while another swept down. As Howard wrote that morning, "Their force is wonderfully great and strong, yet we pluck

their feathers by little and little."

Just when it looked as if all the Spanish ships would be wrecked on the banks of Zeeland, the wind shifted to the south-west, enabling them to limp northwards. "There was never anything which pleased me better," wrote Drake, "than seeing the enemy flying with a southerly wind to the northwards. I doubt not but ere it be long so to handle the matter with the Duke of Sidonia as he shall wish himself at Cadiz among his orange trees."

The end of the Armada

The weather did the rest. Pursued as far as the Scottish border, where lack of ammunition and food forced the English to turn back, the battered Spanish galleons had no choice but to continue northabout round Scotland and Ireland, their leaking hulls riddled with shot holes, their rigging cut to pieces, their water casks empty, and with little food left after the English had denied them the opportunity to replenish their stores at Calais.

Once more they encountered another gale of that tempestuous summer. Ship after ship was driven ashore on the Outer Hebrides, or wrecked on the western coast of Ireland. As their officers struggled through the surf, they were set upon and robbed and often murdered. Others, sheltered by Catholic priests, escaped inland.

The wrecks of twenty-five galleons lie off the Irish coast. Sidonia kept another fifty together until they were scattered by yet another storm in the Bay of Biscay. He is described as sitting with his head between his hands until the remnant of his fleet reached Santander, where the boys in the streets mocked him with cries of "Drake is coming!" He had lost fifty-five ships in all, and a third of the men who had sailed three months before.

Queen Elizabeth gave scant credit to her seamen when she ordered a medal to be struck to commemorate the event with the words, "God blew with his winds and they were scattered." Undoubtedly the storms caused the wrecks, but had it not been for the damage done to the ships at Gravelines most of the Armada might have returned home in safety.

The Anglo-Spanish war dragged on until the end of the reign, but Spanish power declined steadily after 1588. For the English, the victory over the Armada was a vision that their future lay upon the seas.

Elizabethan seaman
with astrolabe under
his arm

CHAPTER 4

THE FOUR DAYS' BATTLE

During the first half of the seventeenth century Spanish power was in decline, the English navy neglected and the French hardly yet built. It was therefore possible for the Dutch, once they had won their independence, to develop into the leading maritime nation with astonishing speed.

The basis of their prosperity was their fishing fleet in the North Sea, consisting of 2,000 trawlers called *schuyts* or *busses*. By building a cheap and commodious type of cargo carrier called a *fluyt*, they gained control of the Baltic trade as well as that of the Mediterranean. Outside Europe they conquered an empire in the Spice Islands which proved richer and more lasting than that of Spain in America. Dutch East Indiamen, the largest vessels afloat, traded with Canton and even Japan, where no other European nation was permitted. In the West Indies they took possession of two rich little islands, and there was a group of colonies around New York on the American mainland.

To hold this maritime empire together and to carry the immense quantity of goods which made Holland the magazine of European trade, they became expert shipbuilders and map-makers. In the field of art, the Golden Age of Holland included not only Rembrandt and Vermeer but the

Departure of a Dutch East Indiaman

Willem Van de Velde,
the marine artist

best marine artists who have ever lived—Willem Van de Velde and his son. They have left a wonderfully accurate record of their times, because the father was accredited by Admiral De Ruyter as the first war correspondent to row around the fleet and record his actions during his wars with England.

Such wars were bound to occur, since both seafaring nations depended on overseas trade for their existence. When the Grand Pensionary (first minister of Holland and Zeeland), John de Witt, said that "the Hollanders have well nigh beaten all nations, by traffic, out of the seas, and become the only carrier of goods throughout the world," his boast was almost justified. When the governor of the Spice Islands massacred English merchants (thereby diverting the attention of their successors to India itself) nothing was done about it. When Admiral Marten Tromp defeated a Spanish Armada within sight of the English coast, the English fleet did not dare to intervene.

England looks to her defences

With the coming of Oliver Cromwell everything changed. Just as he had defeated the Royalists in the Civil War with his New Model Army, so he was now determined to protect his country's interests with a new navy. The first step was to pass the Navigation Act, which forbade English cargoes to be shipped in foreign vessels. The next was to send some of his generals to sea to command the powerful new warships he was building.

Of these Generals-at-Sea, as they were called (the word "admiral" still being usually applied to a ship, not a man), the most important were Robert Blake and George Monck. In order to create an efficient fleet, Blake insisted that the time had come to differentiate between a merchant ship and a warship. Three-deckers ·mounting a hundred guns were now being built. Even the great East Indiamen were not so strong, because if they carried more than a few guns there would be no room left for their cargoes.

Building a Dutch
East Indiaman

A new model navy

Not only was it important to build and arm specialized warships but there must be strict discipline on board and an agreed method of tactics and signals to fight them. So, at Blake's suggestion, a naval disciplinary code was formulated known as the Articles of War, and a code of tactics began with the Fighting Instructions. These laid down the mode of attack, the admiral in the centre firing a gun and hoisting a particular flag in a given position to signify which Instruction was to be put into force. Furthermore, since fleets were now so huge and unwieldy, they were organized into three divisions, each under an admiral whose flag at the foremast was of a distinguishing colour. Thus in the English navy (and other navies soon copied the arrangement) the Admiral of the Fleet flew a red flag in his flagship in the centre; his vice-admiral flew a white flag in the van; his rear-admiral flew a blue flag in command of the rear squadron.

Naval warfare was thus becoming organized, just as the warship was becoming a special type of ship rated according to the number of guns she carried. A first rate line-of-battle ship carried ninety or a hundred guns on three decks. The second rates were two-deckers with

Sovereign of the Seas and her builder Peter Pett

Using a cross-staff

39

English man-of-war becalmed, by Van de Velde

seventy or eighty, the third rates carried sixty or over. These big ships composed the line of battle, whereas single decked frigates (as they later came to be called) were too weak to lie in the line during a fleet action; they were used for scouting, convoy protection or commerce destruction. In order to bring their full fire power into play, war-ships now fought in *line ahead,* each fleet passing on opposite tacks, then turning about to deliver another broadside as they passed each other. The revolution in tactics from the *line abreast* formation in which galleys fought was at last complete.

All these developments occurred during the three Anglo-Dutch wars

in 1652-4, 1664-7, 1672-4. The English led the way because at first the Dutch navy was not as strong as her merchant marine; but it soon caught up. Thus the English emerged victorious from the First War, but not from the Second, and the Dutch were only defeated in the Third because they were attacked by land as well as by sea.

First round to England

The First War consisted largely of duels between Blake and Tromp in which first one side and then the other claimed the victory. All the battles were fought between the coasts of Holland and England or in the Channel, and they all had the same character of vast fleets cannonading away, seldom coming to grips with each other but drifting in clouds of smoke as the seamen-gunners fought it out, often for days on end. Now it was Tromp defeating Blake off Dungeness and (according to legend) hoisting a broom at his masthead to show that he had driven the English off the sea. A few months later it was Blake harrying Tromp off Portland as the latter skilfully protected a convoy by fighting a rearguard action until it reached home. In the last battle of the war Tromp was killed and the English blockaded the Dutch coast "as 'twere be-sieged."

The Dutch suffered from two weaknesses which in the end proved fatal, in spite of the skill and resolution of their leaders. Their country lay at the wrong end of the Channel. Depending for their life-blood on the arrival of merchant vessels from their overseas empire, they were at the mercy of the English once the latter could establish a stranglehold on the Channel highway and cut their life-line. Furthermore, since the United Netherlands was a federation, each of the seven provinces had its own admiralty, so that the organization of national fleets was a complicated and unsatisfactory business.

A see-saw struggle

Nevertheless, in the Second War the Dutch navy reached its climax of efficiency under Marten Tromp's

George Monck, Earl of Albemarle

Cornelis Tromp

Michiel de Ruyter

Samuel Pepys
Sir William Penn

James II
Prince Rupert

son, Cornelis, and Michiel Adrians-zoon De Ruyter, the greatest sea-man of the century. Blake was dead, but Monck, over sixty years old, was now Duke of Albemarle, because he changed sides in politics and brought Charles II back to the throne. Since Charles had spent his exile in Holland, it might be thought that the two nations would live in peace, but the economic reasons for their rivalry were still unsettled. As Albemarle bluntly put it, "What we want is more of the trade which the Dutch now have." Or, as one of his captains said to Samuel Pepys, the Secretary of the Admiralty and as famous as a bureaucrat as a diarist, "The trade of the world is too little for us two, therefore one must down."

Once more there were many con-fused and hard fought actions between huge fleets of nearly a hundred ships on each side. In the Second Dutch War of 1664-7 the Dutch were better led and equipped, and the English suffered a perpetual lack of cash because Parliament distrusted the king and never under-stood the needs of the navy.

In the first major clash off Lowestoft the king's brother, James, Duke of York (later James II) and Admiral Sir William Penn, father of the Quaker founder of Pennsylvania, defeated the Dutch under Opdam when his flagship exploded and he lost his life, together with those of five hundred men. But the longest and hardest of the battles, known as the Four Days Battle because it began off the Dutch coast on 1st June 1666, and ended at the mouth of the Thames on 4th June, was a Dutch victory, if the reckoning is made in the number of ships and men lost.

The English started by making the mistake of dividing their forces. Because of a rumour that the French

The Four Days'
Battle, by A. Storck

(now in strange alliance with Holland) were sending a fleet up Channel, Prince Rupert was despatched with twenty-four ships in a westerly direction. Meanwhile Albemarle with sixty ships came upon the Dutch fleet of ninety in thick weather nine miles off Dunkirk. "The general," writes an eyewitness, "called immediately a council of flag officers, which being done, the sign was put out to fall into line of battle."

This was by now the normal formation. How impressive it was is described by a Frenchman serving in the Dutch fleet: "Nothing equals the beautiful order of the English at sea. Never was a line drawn straighter than that formed by their ships; thus they bring all their fire to bear upon those who draw near

them. They fight like a line of cavalry which is handled according to rule; whereas the Dutch advance like cavalry whose squadrons leave their ranks and come separately to the charge."

In order to avoid the English attack, Tromp cut his anchor cables and made for the open sea. De Ruyter followed him in his huge flagship, the *Seven Provinces,* longing to avenge the defeat of the previous year. Out at sea the waves were so high that the English could not open their lower gunports, and they were also outnumbered in ships. It is said that when the *Swiftsure* was taken, the prisoners cried for mercy, "Pardon, messieurs! Pardon, messieurs!", voluntarily stripping off their clothes in token of surrender. The captain of the

Using a back-staff

The Dutch flagship Seven Provinces, by Van de Velde

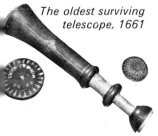

The oldest surviving telescope, 1661

captured Tromp before De Ruyter came to the rescue, reproving the cheering crew with the words, "This is no time for rejoicing, but rather for tears." With so many ships damaged and others deserting him, Albemarle continued his slow retreat towards the English coast.

On the third day he protected his damaged ships by placing his flagship and other big ships in the rear so that De Ruyter could not close. Even then the *Royal Prince* went aground on the Galloper shoal at the mouth of the Thames, where Tromp took possession of her; but he had to burn her to prevent the English retaking her. On board his own flagship, the *Royal Charles,* Albemarle was so closely pressed that he was seen to prime a pocket pistol to blow up the magazine if she was boarded. So, says a courtier who evidently did not take the fighting very seriously, "Mr. Savile and I in a laughing way most mutinously resolved to throw him overboard in case we should catch him going down to the powder room."

Fortunately, in the afternoon there was a cry from the masthead that Rupert's squadron was in sight. The dashing prince had heard the sound of battle and, as always, hastened towards it. His arrival equalized the number of ships still fighting, so that on the morning of the fourth day he led the van in another attack, but before he could close with his pursuers his topmast was shot away.

Both sides were now running short of ammunition after such a long and damaging struggle. Even De Ruyter confessed that he could not continue: "So many ships were heavily damaged, especially in the rigging, and many had run short of powder, so that I decided to break off the engagement and confide the

ship continued the fight until he was killed by a bullet in the throat; he lay so covered in his blood beside the helm that he could not be identified until the men plundering his corpse found a diamond jewel on him. On board the *Henry,* Captain Harman's leg was broken by a falling yard after he had fended off three fire-ships. Admiral Evertzoon called on him to surrender the ship. "No, no," he replied, "it is not come to that yet," and with another broadside killed the Dutch admiral himself.

Fighting went on until nightfall, when the weary crews on both sides fell to rest, knowing well that it would be renewed at dawn. On the second day, though outnumbered worse than before, Albemarle impetuously attacked again. He almost

safety of the fleet to the hazards of the seas." An English account says that in the evening "their Admiral on a sudden fired a gun to call in the straggling remains of his tattered fleet (who were at this time reduced from eighty-four to under the number of forty sail) and bore away before the wind towards Flushing."

It was the hardest fought battle in all three Anglo-Dutch wars. A Frenchman gives a delightful picture of De Ruyter the day after his victory: "Amid all the disorders of the fleet he seemed only to be moved by the misfortune to his country, but always submissive to the Will of God. He had something of the frankness and lack of polish of our patriarchs, and to conclude I will only relate that the day after the victory I found him sweeping his own cabin and feeding his chickens."

His victory was not complete enough to stop the English appearing off the Dutch coast a few weeks later. Nor did he succeed in restoring the balance at the battle of St James's Day (called by the Dutch the Two Days' Battle), when he lost twenty ships. "I wish I were dead," he cried. "I wish the same for me," answered his captain, "but one does not die exactly when one wants to." As the two men left the cabin a shot crashed into it, smashing the table at which they had been sitting. Soon afterwards an attack was made on a huge collection of merchant ships in the Vlie river near Terschelling by Sir Robert Holmes, a notable fire-eater. He burned 165 vessels in what became known as Holmes's Bonfire, and for the first time marines are recorded as having landed to burn the warehouses of the town.

No wonder the Dutch saw in the Great Fire of London later that summer a divine retribution. Having

H.M.S. Resolution in a Gale, *by Van de Velde*

Cherub using quadrant

suffered the Plague the year before, with the Fire of London and the perpetual lack of cash to pay the seamen, the English put out peace feelers, but before negotiations were completed De Ruyter achieved the most brilliant stroke of his career.

He knew that the English fleet was laid up in the Medway river near Chatham after the recent disasters. With great skill he took his own fleet up the Thames, piloted by Englishmen who had deserted for lack of wages. With such sailors shouting, "We have come to get our pay!" he broke the chain across the Medway, silenced the forts, burned the warships and towed home the flagship, the *Royal Charles,* whose marvellously carved and gilded stern may still be seen in the Rijksmuseum at Amsterdam.

CHAPTER 5

BARFLEUR AND THE FRENCH CORSAIRS

The rise of a new French navy was as rapid as that of Holland. When France's greatest bureaucrat, Jean Baptiste Colbert, began to take an interest in naval affairs in 1665 he found only two or three ships fit for service. By the time of his death in 1683 there were 200 and a force of 53,000 seamen, apart from scores of agile privateers from the old corsair ports of Nantes, St Malo and Dunkirk.

An immense effort was made to provide France with the finest navy as well as the finest army in Europe. Arsenals and naval academies were built at Brest and Toulon, because the nature of the country's coastline required a two-ocean navy with fleets in both the Mediterranean and the Atlantic. Intensive training in tactics and signals was undertaken, the textbook (written by a naval chaplain) remaining the standard work on the subject for the next century. All the resources of French science were utilized for ship-building, the resulting masterpieces being lavishly decorated ships of the largest class, the 2,400-ton *Soleil Royal* and the *Royal Louis,* each mounting the unusually high number of 120 guns.

What continued to handicap the navy for a hundred years to come was the fact that the king and his courtiers regarded the army as the senior service, so that a commission in the royal regiments was preferable for aristocrats who disliked uncomfortable conditions at sea. Even those of the nobility who chose the naval profession carried into it all the class snobbery which marred the *ancien régime*. Favoured sons formed the aristocratic *gardes de la marine* (or *rouges* as they were called from the colour of their breeches), who looked down upon the more efficient officers drawn from the merchant service, called the *bleus*. With few exceptions, all the principal posts went to the former. To man the fleet, Colbert invented an elaborate plan for the conscription of all sea-going persons called the *inscription maritime*. It looked well on paper, but it was no more popular or effective than the rough methods of the press gangs in England.

Nevertheless, an impressive navy had been created and, as we have seen, it won its first victories in the Third Dutch War and again when fighting the Dutch in alliance with Spain off Sicily.

A French victory

The first real test came with the outbreak of the War of the English Succession in 1689, when the supporters of the Protestant William of Orange invited him over to replace the Catholic James II. It

H.M.S. Royal Sovereign, *by Van de Velde*

Jean-Baptiste Colbert

Le Comte de Tourville

was James's tragedy that he lost his throne, and failed in his attempt to regain it, because of the fleet of which (as Duke of York) he had once been Lord High Admiral. In 1689 his fleet was wind-bound in the Thames, so that William landed unopposed in the west country. Three years later, when as an exile and a pensioner of Louis XIV he was waiting to invade England from the Cherbourg peninsula, the French fleet was destroyed under his eyes at La Hougue (usually called La Hogue by the English).

In the interval the French navy nearly proved his salvation. He was landed with an army in Ireland, thereby forcing William to hasten thither just when the Dutch frontier fortresses were being attacked by the main French army. Queen Mary was left at the head of the government in London and in 1690 she unwisely ordered Lord Torrington, commander-in-chief. of the allied fleet in the Channel, to give battle.

Nothing could have been more ill-advised. The Comte de Tourville, the most skilful tactician of the age, had entered the Channel with the combined fleets of Toulon and Brest some weeks before he was expected. He had at his disposal seventy-five ships, whereas the Anglo-Dutch fleet (the Dutch division being under the command of the youngest of the Evertzoon family) amounted to only fifty-nine. Letters from Versailles assured him that the eyes of Europe were upon him and that he must show the world what was expected of the new French navy. He did all he could to close with the enemy, but Torrington held him off until he was told to stand and fight.

This he did off Beachy Head on 30th June, 1690. (The French call the battle by the name of Bévéziers, a corruption of the name of the neighbouring town of Pevensey). Tourville's superiority in numbers and his skill in tactics were obvious from the start. It enabled him to "double" or envelop the Dutch van, which was thus cut off from the centre, where the French divided Torrington's over-stretched line.

By noon the allies were in serious difficulties: the rear of both fleets were locked in battle, the centre under Torrington pierced and the Dutch in the van almost surrounded. Then the tide turned. Torrington immediately ordered his ships to anchor. Before Tourville realized what was happening, his own ships were carried so far to the westward that they were out of range. As soon as the tide ebbed in the evening, Torrington hastened to retreat before the French could catch up with him, abandoning six damaged Dutch ships and one English. Once in the Thames, all the buoys were pulled up so that the French could not navigate the river.

When he was tried for his defeat, Torrington gained his aquittal by an interesting defence of his conduct which in time became an important strategic doctrine. "Most men were in fear that the French would invade," he said, "but I was always of another opinion. For I said that whilst we had a fleet in being they would not dare to make the attempt." Right up to the present day, commanders of an inferior but undefeated force have relied on this strategy of "a fleet in being" as a deterrent to invasion operations.

The French had won a notable success in 1690. The next year Tourville flew his flag unchallenged in the Channel. Nevertheless, he did not make good use of his victory, because William was able to ferry troops across to Ireland, where he defeated James at the battle of the Boyne.

In 1692 James, with the support of 30,000 troops provided by Louis XIV and Tourville's victorious fleet, prepared for invasion from the Cherbourg peninsula. It seemed as if the stage was set for another Norman conquest, but Tourville did not want to give battle until his force was big enough to defeat Admiral Russell, now in command of the allied fleet. The king demanded a battle, whatever the odds: "I wish that the order be executed exactly," he wrote in his own hand. Tourville continued to protest that he must have reinforcements. "It is not for you to dispute the king's orders," wrote the Minister of Marine. "You must execute them by entering the Channel. Tell me if you will do so; if not, the king will replace you with someone more obedient and less timid than you are."

This slur on his professional honour spurred Tourville on. At the last moment the government realized the truth of the situation and sent ten despatch boats to stop him, but not one reached him in time. He had already engaged, though he only had forty-four ships, twenty others being left behind at Brest for lack of crews. Russell, on the other hand, had ninety-nine, with the inevitable consequence that the battle off Cape Barfleur on 19th May (29th May by the French calendar), 1692, was the story of the last encounter in reverse.

When the mist cleared that morning, Tourville saw before him a long line of ships, twice his own force in number and so long that he feared he would be outflanked. To avoid this he overstretched his line, so that Sir Cloudesley Shovell was able to penetrate his centre with twenty-five ships. Both centre and rear were soon nearly surrounded, the gigantic *Soleil Royal* at one time

top: Stern of model of H.M.S. Prince *1670*

bottom: Figurehead of H.M.S. Prince *1670*

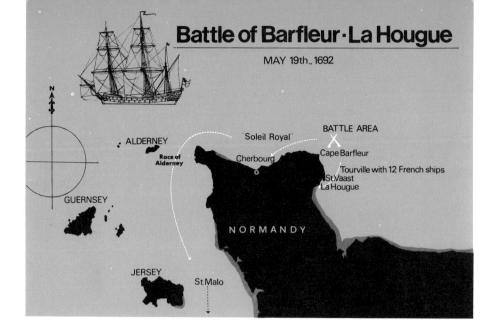

Battle of Barfleur·La Hougue

MAY 19th., 1692

fighting off the attacks of three big English ships. Once more the tide turned at the height of the action, this time in Tourville's favour. The allies were carried eastward out of range, the gallant Shovell having to fight his way back to rejoin the main body through enfilading fire. At midnight the French withdrew, just as Torrington had done two years earlier.

The decisive battle

So far the French had not lost a single ship. By Tourville's skill and courage, the fleet had been extricated from a critical situation. But his retreat was not as easy as that of the allies on the former occasion. Brest was too far away. The only channel to a home port was through the dangerous Race of Alderney leading to St Malo. Twenty ships were sent by this route with the English at their heels. Only the skill and local knowledge of a Breton pilot named Hervé Riel, enabled them to reach safety by a channel which everyone else declared to be unnavigable by large vessels.

The *Soleil Royal* had been so badly damaged when she bore the brunt of the fighting off Barfleur, that Tour-ville sent her to Cherbourg with two other big ships. All three were burned by English fire-ships as they lay at anchor. The remaining twelve were taken by Tourville to La Hogue, a few miles south of Cape Barfleur (where American forces landed in 1944). From this beach and the neighbouring St Vaast, James was intending to launch his invasion. On May 24th Russell's ships came into view. He could not take them into the shallow water where the French had run themselves aground. He therefore sent Admiral George Rooke with two hundred small boats covered by the guns of frigates to destroy them under the eyes of James and the troops encamped on the cliffs above. At one point French cavalry tried to intervene by riding into the surf, but the English sailors knew their business and one by one the French warships were set ablaze.

New strategy

This battle of La Hogue was called by the historian, Michelet, one of the decisive battles of the world, because it marked the end of Colbert's navy. It was the Trafalgar of the seventeenth century. The *Grand Mon-*

arque was so disgusted that he turned all his resources to his armies. Hence there were few big fleet actions during the remainder of the war, nor during the War of the Spanish Succession which followed it. Instead, there developed a far more dangerous type of warfare, as far as the English were concerned. It relied on the genius and enterprise of the wolves of the sea, the corsairs of St Malo and Dunkirk. It was a war to destroy English and Dutch commerce in the same way as Drake and the Elizabethan privateers had a century before tried to destroy Spanish trade. It was a war in which sea heroes surrounded by legend (as Drake had been) appeared from the humble ranks of the privateers, whose names are better known to-day than any of those of the admirals of Louis XIV.

Privateering was then a perfectly legitimate form of warfare. If commissioned by a government with what were called letters of marque, a privately owned armed vessel was not in the same category as a pirate, however similar their methods. What was required was a daring captain, acting on his own account, able to snap up merchant vessels straying from a convoy, or foolishly sailing independently, trusting to her size or her proximity to a friendly coast. In the last quarter of the century thousands of such traders and fishing vessels were taken by the corsairs of St Malo and Dunkirk, both towns being well situated at either end of the Channel and both breeding the best seamen France has ever produced. Such men soon became folk heroes. They were unsuited for the more disciplined life on board royal warships. They lived by their wits and their daring, preying on the life-blood of their enemies.

There is no space here to deal with more than two such corsairs, nor to describe their methods of fighting, which in any case—as in all small single-ship actions—were much the same. It was a matter of surprise, fine seamanship and ability to handle small, fast vessels; above all, an audacity to attack bigger ships which were often heavily armed escorting warships. It was always a case of getting to windward of an enemy, closing, grappling, boarding and fighting it out hand to hand. It was seldom a question of trying to sink a vessel by gunfire, or of attacking in groups of more than two or three: it was the value of the prize, not the destruction of the enemy, which mattered to such men.

Bow of model of
Soleil Royal

Sea wolves

Jean Bart of Dunkirk came of corsair stock, his grandfather being known as the Sea Fox. He served under De Ruyter as a boy, and he took part in the attack on the English in the Medway. He became the youthful hero of Dunkirk when he captured thirty-two vessels in his twenty-four gun *Palme* which had a crew of 150 men. He is described as tall, strong, daring, crafty and almost illiterate. One story tells how he lashed his young son to the mast when he showed signs of fear, crying, "It is necessary that he should get accustomed to this sort of music." Another tells how, when asked by a circle of courtiers at Versailles how he managed to get to sea when the English were blockading him, he replied by raising his elbows and using his fists to break through them—"that's the way I did it." According to his corsair companion Forbin (an excellent seaman but very much the fine gentleman who despised his companion in arms), it was the fashion at court to "go and pay a visit to the Chevalier de Forbin and his *bear*."

So many legends surrounded Jean Bart's career that it is difficult to come at the truth. There is no doubt that when in 1689 he commanded the *Railleuse* (twenty-four guns) and *Serpente* (sixteen)—both provided for him by the Minister of Marine—he captured the Dutch frigate *Seahorse* in spite of her fifty guns and took nine ships out of her convoy; or that he and Forbin landed on the English coast near Newcastle; or again that he fought a pitched battle with eight Dutch warships in order to bring a convoy of grain ships into port, together with three captured frigates. Both he and Forbin were taken prisoner by the English frigate *Nonsuch* and sent to Plymouth, where they escaped by a rope over a wall, seized a fishing boat in the harbour and made their way to St Malo. Both men served in Tourville's fleet, but the life of a captain of a royal ship was not to their taste. Bart died of pleurisy in 1702, his name being commemorated in many ships of later date, including a battleship.

Duguay-Trouin, his younger contemporary, was the hero of St Malo. If ever there was a town which

Capture of a French privateer Comte de Toulouse *in 1703*

Jean Bart

lived by the sea, it was this, and the fame of Malouin privateers was well known long before his day. They were freebooters in the West Indies and scores of them actually circumnavigated the world, though few were literate enough to leave a record of their voyages. In peacetime they were either smugglers or buccaneers; in wartime they were formidable corsairs.

Duguay-Trouin went to sea at the age of eighteen in 1689. Two years later he was given the command of a small vessel by a St Malo shipbuilder. He spent most of his career cruising around Ireland, or in the Bristol Channel, where he once took two West Indian vessels loaded with sugar. In the Scilly Islands he was caught by five warships, sent to prison at Plymouth like Bart, and like him escaped in an open boat to St Malo. By a remarkable coincidence he captured the *Nonsuch* frigate in 1696, the same ship which had taken Bart seven years previously. He renamed her the *Sanspareil* and continued his marauding career through both the early Anglo-French wars.

The relation of these men to the navy is not easy to define. Most of them were commissioned as naval officers after their early successes and from time to time served on board royal warships. Their own ships were often provided, paid for and armed by the Minister of Marine or the Minister of War, whose advice (had the king taken it) was to fit out flotillas of such privateers from Dunkirk. Moreover, since French strategy was now a war on commerce, there were many occasions on which naval ships captured merchant vessels just as privateers did. On the most notable of such occasions, Tourville's fleet intercepted a huge English convoy from Smyrna in the Levant, captured eighty-four vessels and caused many a bankruptcy in the city of London.

The only answer to such a form of warfare (as it has proved the answer to the submarine of modern times) was to compel merchant ships to sail in convoy escorted by warships, usually frigates and sloops. Throughout the next century, however, the Dunkirkers and the Malouins continued their depredations on English shipping, and their example was later followed by American privateers. There was wealth as well as fame to be won in this exciting form of warfare, and when it was over many a privateer turned easily enough into a pirate.

Section of a first-rate ship

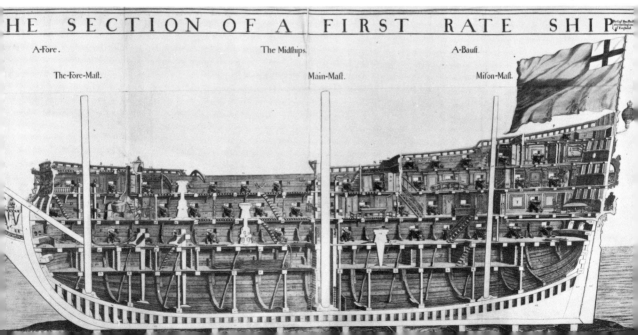

THE SECTION OF A FIRST RATE SHIP

A-Fore.   The Midships.   A-Baust.

The-Fore-Mast.   Main-Mast.   Mison-Mast.

CHAPTER 6

QUIBERON BAY

The chief object of the many wars fought between France and Britain from 1689 to the downfall of Napoleon in 1815 was the prize of empire and overseas trade. With her larger population and more efficient army, France usually tried to decide the issue by land warfare and by schemes for the invasion of the British Isles which never came to anything. Britain preferred the sea and after much trial and error evolved a maritime strategy which succeeded in the end.

In this long struggle, strategy proved more important than tactics; that is to say, it was of more consequence to decide where to station fleets and what conquests might be made by means of amphibious expeditions overseas than to depend on the result of a battle at sea. The reason was that by this date tactics under sail had been perfected to a point where a decisive victory was impossible unless some accident occurred. If correctly handled, and provided the numbers on both sides were more or less equal, so that conterminous lines of battle could be formed, there was nothing except a sudden change of wind or a disastrous collision which could alter the balance of power between them.

As a French admiral said, encounters between two equal fleets

Battle of Quiberon Bay

55

now resembled the movements in a ballet. Each side bombarded the other as their lines passed on opposite tacks, but until things changed towards the end of the century they never destroyed each other. The formalism of the age of the minuet was reflected in the tactics of its fleets. The only possibility of a real victory was when such formalities were abandoned and a battle took the form of a chase in which the retreating fleet was driven on the rocks. That is what happened at the battle of Quiberon Bay in 1759.

The struggle for empire

At the beginning of the century, France and Britain were equally placed in their rivalry for empire overseas. In North America there was New France, or Canada, with English colonies strung along the Atlantic seaboard. The West Indies were about equally divided. In India, the East India Companies of both nations held similar positions as trading posts: the era of expansion, planned by Dupleix and achieved by Robert Clive, had not yet begun.

What, in the long run, upset the balance of power was the British strategy of blockading French fleets in their European ports, while sending expeditions overseas to conquer enemy colonies, the garrisons of which could not be reinforced from home. It was during the Seven Years' War (1756–63), under the guidance of William Pitt, Earl of Chatham, that this essentially maritime strategy worked best.

Yet the war started badly for Britain when their base in the Mediterranean, at Minorca, was captured by the Duc de Richelieu. Admiral Byng failed to drive off the French fleet from Toulon and he was shot for his failure—*"pour encourager les autres,"* said Voltaire. Then Pitt came to power and with Lord Anson at the Admiralty put into practice the true principles of maritime strategy. By sending money to his ally, Frederick the Great of Prussia, he kept the French

Admiral Lord Anson, by Sir Joshua Reynolds

and Austrian armies engaged in Germany. Since the King of England was also Elector of Hanover, a British army was sent there to win the battle of Minden. But the main concentration was in the direction of Canada, India and the West Indies, while French fleets were blockaded in Europe.

In the year 1759 this strategy was wonderfully successful. General James Wolfe was taken up the St. Lawrence river to Quebec by Admiral Saunders and on the Heights of Abraham defeated the Marquis de Montcalm. In the same

Lord George Graham in his cabin by Hogarth, painted before officers wore uniforms

A British seaman

LE DUC DE BOURGOGNE,

VÜE DU VAISSEAU DU ROY
Lancé a la Mer dans le Port
de Rochefort le 20 Octobre 1751.

Launching of
Le Duc de Bourgogne
at Rochefort 1751

Admiral
Sir Edward Hawke

way, Guadaloupe and Martinique were later taken by amphibious expeditions, while Clive was enabled to conquer large parts of India by the assistance he received from Admiral Watson in the Bay of Bengal.

The British blockade

All these successes depended on a strong guard being kept over the French fleets in Europe to prevent any help being sent to their beleaguered garrisons. Admiral Boscawen was stationed at Gibraltar to prevent the Toulon fleet reaching the Atlantic. When they tried to do so in August, 1759, he soundly defeated them off Lagos.

The main British fleet (now called the Channel Fleet) was used to guard Brest. This was under the command of Sir Edward Hawke, who evolved a most efficient system of blockade to keep the door securely locked. In addition to his main body of line-of-battle ships off Ushant, he had an inshore squadron of smaller ships watching the approaches to Brest, with a force of frigates which could ride out a storm in Douarnenez Bay under Captain Duff, to patrol farther south.

The fleet was supplied by a host of small victuallers from Plymouth, and if a westerly gale blew up it could retire two hundred miles north to shelter in Torbay, since Hawke was confident that as long as the wind blew directly on shore the French could not get out. In normal weather, day in and day out, in winter and summer, Hawke's ships sailed up and down guarding Brest. Sometimes they came so close inshore that Breton peasants could see the men on their decks. Sometimes they disappeared over the horizon in the direction of Ushant. Only when a westerly gale threatened to blow them onto the coast did they relinquish their station.

An ill-fated plan

The only counter-plan which Louis XV could devise was to invade

England with an army gathered in Brittany sailing under the protection of the Brest fleet. But how was that fleet to get out? Their sole chance was the short interval between the time Hawke was driven off station by a gale and the time he returned. It was a very risky scheme. When it had to be postponed to a stormy November it was doomed.

All the summer, troops had been collecting at Vannes under the command of the Duc d'Aguillon, who had made his reputation by repelling an English landing at St Malo. They were to embark in the Morbihan, a rock-strewn bay east of the Quiberon peninsula. The Brest fleet, under the Comte de Conflans, was to seize the opportunity of Hawke's temporary absence to slip out and pick up the troops. Conflans was a marshal of France with little experience at sea; he was old and sick.

So things stood during the long hot summer of 1759. On the whole, Hawke's fleet was well supplied from Plymouth, though he was always complaining that the beer turned sour and the bread was so full of weevils that it had to be thrown overboard. Until 9th November he never left his station, but then a westerly gale blew up and he was forced to go north. At that season of the year he never expected that the invasion plan would be attempted; in any case, Captain Duff had been left to give warning if Conflans escaped.

He was only away ten days, but that was time enough for a French force of seven big ships to get into Brest to help the whole fleet of twenty-one ships of the line to escape from their land-locked harbour and begin the short voyage south to Quiberon. Conflans had two hundred miles start of Hawke when he got out.

On 19th November the latter was back off Ushant when two of his supply ships told him that they had seen the French fleet south-east of Belle Isle. Duff, who knew nothing about their escape, was almost

Captain Keppel

Launching of 100-gun ship at Deptford

caught on the morning of the 20th, but at that very moment there were shouts from the mastheads of the French ships that a big fleet could be seen approaching under press of sail from the west.

Conflans decided to run for it, leading his ships in the eighty-gun *Soleil Royal*, because he was sure that with a strong wind blowing on shore from the west no enemy would dare to follow him into the dangerous waters of the Morbihan. The English had no pilots, nor charts. They could hardly come up with him before darkness fell on that stormy November afternoon. No admiral, he said, would risk his ships among the rocks and shoals of that bay under such conditions.

Nevertheless, Hawke signalled General Chase by firing his signal gun three times and hoisting a white flag with a red cross on it at the top-masthead of his flagship, the *Royal George*. That meant that there was to be no strict formation like a line of battle, but that every ship must race as fast as possible to catch up with the rear of the enemy. As he told his officers, "he was of the old way of fighting, to make down-right work with them"; that is to say, he intended to revert to the days before formal tactics developed.

Rock-strewn waters

The *Royal George* was three miles astern of the rearmost French ship when this signal was made. Just as Conflans was entering Quiberon Bay, between Le Four shoal and the Cardinal rocks, with Belle Isle a mile or two to the west, the leading British ships—*Torbay*, *Resolution* and *Warspite*—opened fire at half past two in the afternoon. The red flag of battle was now streaming from the flagship's foremast, signifying that "every ship is to use their utmost endeavour to engage the enemy as close as possible." Hawke, of course, made for the *Soleil Royal*. When his navigating officer pointed out that "if we run on much longer, sir, we must run

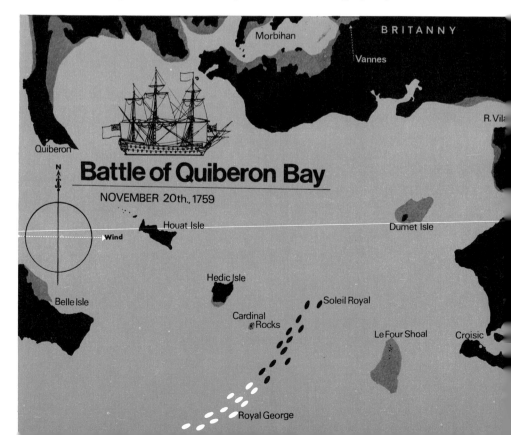

Morbihan

BRITANNY

Vannes

R. Vila

Quiberon

Battle of Quiberon Bay

NOVEMBER 20th., 1759

N

Houat Isle

Dumet Isle

Wind

Hedic Isle

Belle Isle

Soleil Royal

Cardinal Rocks

Le Four Shoal

Croisic

Royal George

Quiberon Bay,
French ship on the
rocks

on shore," Hawke replied, "That may be, but they must be on shore first, so lay me alongside the *Soleil Royal*."

By this time there was only an hour of daylight left. Over forty big ships were veering and tacking in a high wind with rocks and shoals surrounding them. There were many collisions. There was no distinguishing friend from foe unless someone caught sight of a flag, or the whole side of a ship suddenly burst into flames with a broadside.

A sudden squall laid the *Thesée* (seventy-four guns) on her beam end. She sank with the loss of six hundred lives, only twenty-two survivors being picked up the next morning by the *Torbay*. After suffering four hundred casualties from the concentrated fire of the *Magnanime* which was at this time a British ship under Captain Richard Howe (who, thirty years later, was to win the victory of the Glorious First of June) but eleven years previously had been a French warship, the *Héros* surrendered and was burned. The eighty-gun *Formidable* was taken as a prize. On her way to engaging the French flagship, the *Royal George* sank the *Superbe* with one tremendous broadside. There was a feeble cheer as she began to settle because, says her chaplain, "the honest sailors were touched at the fate of so many hundreds of poor creatures."

As darkness fell, Hawke found

Building a 70-gun ship at Deptford

himself engaged with a dozen ships clustered round the *Soleil Royal*. "Night was now come," he wrote after the battle, "and being on a part of the coast among islands and shoals, of which we were totally ignorant, without a pilot, and the wind blowing hard on a lee shore, I made the signal to anchor"—within sight of the steeples of Le Croisic, as he found the next morning. Conflans also anchored, to find himself at dawn in the middle of the English fleet.

So, on the morning of the 21st, the two flagships lay within range of each other. Conflans made straight for the coast, ran his ship on shore, and escaped with most of his crew. The only part of her which Hawke's men could take off was her huge carved figurehead. She was the second flagship of that name to end ignominiously in flames on shore.

During that terrible night two British ships—*Essex* and *Resolution*—had also run aground in the general confusion of wind and darkness. Both were abandoned and burned. The French fleet was scattering in all directions. Seven of the big ships and four frigates made for the mouth of the river Vilaine, the bar of which they only succeeded in crossing by heaving their guns overboard to lighten ship. One grounded and broke her back. Another was wrecked at the mouth of the river Loire. Seven ships were lost in all, with 25,000 men, but a large group escaped south in the direction of Rochefort. It was, indeed, the grave of the navy of Louis XV.

Year of victories

Hawke was as surprised as anyone at the extent of his victory. In his

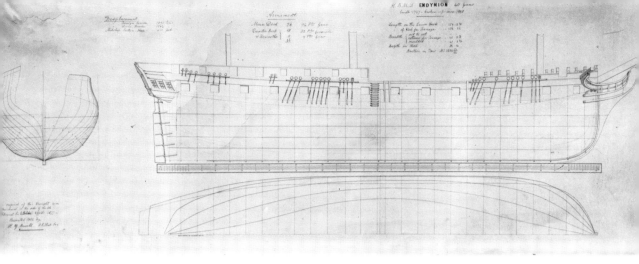

despatch there is a remarkably modest sentence which summarizes the whole story: "When I consider the season of the year, the hard gales on the day of action, a flying enemy, the shortness of the day, and the coast they were on, I can boldly affirm that all that could possibly be done has been done."

London, of course, went wild with joy. By a strange coincidence, the body of General Wolfe was buried at Greenwich the same day as Admiral Hawke crowned the successes of that wonderful year, the Year of Victories, as it came to be called. The toast of the town was: "May all our commanders have the eye of a Hawke and the heart of a Wolfe."

To celebrate the year, David Garrick, the actor, composed a song which has now become a sort of naval anthem:

Hearts of oak are our ships,
Jolly tars are our men;
We always are ready:
Steady, boys, steady:
We'll fight and we'll conquer again
  and again.

Draught of 40-gun frigate Endymion

An English ship blown up by a Frenchman

CHAPTER 7

AMERICAN INDEPENDENCE

Maritime empire depends on the command of the sea. When such command is lost, it inevitably collapses. That is what happened when the colonists along the seaboard of North America rebelled against the mother country only eleven years after Britain had emerged victorious from the Seven Years' War. As long as the American colonists were fighting on their own, the issue remained in doubt; but as soon as the French, and later the Spanish and Dutch as well, entered on their side, the British hold on her American colonies was doomed as soon as she lost command of the seas.

When the struggle began there was, of course, at that time no American navy; but there were hundreds of hardy privateers ready to prey on British shipping returning from the West Indies by the Gulf Stream route. Congress bought four ships, but they were all captured or sunk before the French entered the war in 1778. On board the *Alfred,* however, the largest of these ships, a certain young seaman, Paul Jones, later to become famous, was commissioned as a lieutenant.

He plays the same part in the history of his country's navy as Drake does in that of Britain, or Jean Bart in that of France. Like them, he was a man of humble birth who won fame by striking successes

Paul Jones capturing the Serapis

65

Paul Jones

time. In 1775 he became a lieutenant on board the *Alfred*. Two years later he was given the independent command of the sloop *Ranger* to cross the Atlantic in order to harry British merchant vessels as a commerce destroyer, or, in fact, as a privateer, though he held a commission in the American navy, which provided his ship for him.

Privateer par excellence

Like dozens of other Americans, in 1778 he was cruising in the Irish Sea and the English Channel. He made daring raids on coasts which he knew well, but his exploits in command of this sloop were not very different from those of any other privateer.

However, in 1779, through the good offices of Benjamin Franklin, the unofficial American ambassador at Paris, he got hold of an old East Indiaman which he called *Bonhomme Richard* after one of Franklin's popular books translated under the title of *Le Livre du Bonhomme Richard* (a book which originated the famous *Saturday Evening Post* magazine). She was a big vessel, old and slow, but armed with forty guns and with a crew of 380 men. Jones was once called "a man to be obeyed." Her crew certainly needed such a captain, because they were a mixed lot of adventurers—seventy-nine Americans, fifty-nine Englishmen (mostly deserters), twenty-nine Portuguese, twenty-one Irish, 137 French marines and an odd lot of other nationalities. Such cosmopolitan crews were typical of privateers. What distinguished Jones's crew was the strong body of French marines provided by the new ally of the United States, which also provided two frigates, the *Alliance* (Captain Pierre Landais) and the *Pallas*, all sailing under the "Stars and Stripes" flag.

made on his own account. Like them, he was the sort of man about whom legends gather. Little is known about his early life beyond the fact that he was born in Scotland and went to sea in the West Indies trade, sometimes as a slaver, sometimes in the sugar trade. His name at his birth in 1747 was John Paul, which for some reason he changed to that of Paul Jones. He was certainly brought up in the hardest of schools at sea, so that he grew up tough, independent, brutal and courageous.

His older brother, William, had a small estate in Fredericksburg, Virginia. When William died on the eve of the American Revolution, Paul Jones went to Fredericksburg to live on the estate. But he was soon caught up in the turmoils of the

A bid for glory

Sailing from Lorient in Brittany, Jones decided to search for prizes north of Ireland and Scotland. Having met with little success, he came south to Leith, the port of Edinburgh, and then on down the English coast towards Hull. On 23rd September, 1779, he encountered a large convoy of vessels from the Baltic off Flamborough Head, between Hull and Newcastle. The vessels were escorted by a big new frigate, the forty-four-gun *Serapis,* commanded by Captain Richard Pearson. She was new and copper-bottomed, the practice of coppering the hulls of warships to increase their speed having just been introduced. She was more than a match for the *Bonhomme Richard,* in spite of the latter's size. Yet Jones determined to attack her. He signalled the *Alliance* to support him, but Captain Landais preferred to stand aside and pick up any prizes he could. The *Pallas* accounted for the small armed vessel which accompanied the British frigate, but then did nothing. Like the crowd of spectators on the cliffs of Flamborough Head, her crew had a good view of the fireworks that night (since the action did not begin until dusk), but they could not tell what was happening.

Pearson approached the enemy in the usual way, demanding to know her name, since these strange ships were flying British colours. Jones replied with an imaginary name. "Where from?" queried Pearson. No reply. "Answer immediately, or I shall fire on you." Jones struck his false colours and ran up an enormous American ensign. At the same time he gave the order to fire.

After the second salvo two of his guns burst. A broadside from the English frigate tore into his side.

Captain Pearson

*The action off
Flamborough Head,
Serapis on left*

Paul Jones threatening a sailor

eternity; but let us do our duty." And with his own hands he lashed the forestay of the *Serapis* to the mizzen mast of the *Bonhomme Richard*.

The old ship was being knocked to pieces by the lower-tier guns of the frigate. The carpenter cried out that she was sinking. The gunner rushed to haul down the flag. The captain's reaction was to knock him down with the butt of his pistol. The ship was on fire in several places. Jones sat down for a moment on a hen-coop to recover from exhaustion. Another sailor rushed up to him begging him, for God's sake, to surrender. "No," replied Jones, "I will sink. I will never strike!"

His boarders were already gaining the upper hand in the fighting on the enemy's deck. One man crawled out along the yard of the mainmast with a bucket full of grenades. He threw one down the mainhatch, where it exploded among a heap of cartridges. A hundred prisoners taken from earlier prizes were released on board the *Bonhomme Richard* and might easily have taken command of the ship, had not Jones ordered them to man the pumps.

Within a few minutes the *Serapis* was in a raking position across her bows. "Has your ship struck?" asked Pearson, thinking all was now over. Jones then made the immortal reply: "I have not yet begun to fight."

Realizing that his old ship could not long withstand the heavy fire from the *Serapis*, Jones tried to grapple. Fortunately for him, his jib-boom got entangled with the mizzen rigging of the frigate. "Well done, my brave lads," he shouted, "we've got her now. Throw on board the grappling irons and stand by for boarding." As the master began to swear at the men to make them hurry, he added; "Mr. Stacey, it's no time to be swearing now—you may by the next moment be in

Triumph to tragedy

Meanwhile the *Alliance* had been cruising around, firing on friend and foe alike, but her presence alarmed Captain Pearson. When he found his upper deck held by the enemy, and his mainmast about to go over-board, he surrendered his ship.

It was half past ten at night. Jones had only just enough time to transfer from his old ship when she sank. A few days later he proudly sailed the *Serapis* into the Texel as a prize, with the American ensign flying over the English one. There the fame of his action inspired a song which is still popular, as is the dance named after

his habit of taking prizes. In Paris he was given a sword of honour. He had reached the pinnacle of his fame.

The remainder of his career is tragic. The man whom some have called the father of the U.S. Navy never again commanded a ship, owing to the jealousy of rivals in America. He took service in the navy of Catherine the Great of Russia, where he was called Kontradmiral Pavel Ivanovich Jones, but his appointment was resented by the many English officers already there. He returned to Paris, where he died in poverty, forgotten by his countrymen. It was a hundred years later when his body was brought back to the Naval Academy at Annapolis and his fame was disinterred from the legends which surrounded it.

The penalty of neglect

The fate of great empires, however, is not decided by single ship actions. What ensured the victory of the colonists was the intervention of France, followed by that of Spain and Holland, all seeking revenge on the country which had taken so many of their overseas possessions from them. It was the only war on a world scale which Britain has fought without allies. The American rebellion deprived her of timber and other naval supplies, as well as a source for many prime seamen. Dutch intervention made access to the Baltic difficult. Privateers harassed her trade. Well-conducted French fleets operated in the Caribbean and in the Indian Ocean. Her government was so unpopular with large sections of the people that many officers refused to serve under Lord Sandwich at the Admiralty. Her fleet had been neglected since the end of the last

H.M.S. Royal George

Figurehead of model of Royal George

Stern of model of Royal George *with gun ports open*

De Grasse, and above all the Bailly de Suffren—were some of the best tacticians ever produced in France.

Such tactics were defensive in character. Guns were fired on the up roll of the ship to destroy the masts and rigging of the enemy. Having thus paralysed their opponents, their fleets bore up before the wind and retired to fight another day. The British, on the other hand, preferred more offensive, close range methods, with their guns firing into the hulls of enemy ships. But if the opposing fleet was well manœuvred, if their line of battle held taut, they were not permitted to come within close range. Of course, French tactics never enabled them to win a battle at sea, but if the strategy was correct they could win a campaign or even a war.

Once the hinge of the close blockade of Brest was broken and the door was left open for French fleets to cross the Atlantic, command of the sea was lost. This is what happened when Keppel failed to defeat D'Orvilliers seventy miles off Ushant in 1778. From that time onward the Brest fleet ranged the Channel, or reached the valuable sugar colonies in the West Indies, at will.

George Washington always realized that only with French help could he defeat the British. "In any operations," he told the French government, "and under all circumstances, a decisive naval superiority is to be considered as a fundamental principle, and the basis upon which every hope of success must ultimately depend." He therefore asked not only for troops under the Marquis de Lafayette but for ships and supplies as well.

It was a year before Louis XVI paid attention to him, because the safety of the French West Indies came first. Several fleet actions took

war, and it is significant that Hawke's flagship, the *Royal George,* sank at her moorings merely because her timbers were so rotten that the bottom of the ship fell out.

France's new fleet, on the other hand, was a model of efficiency. The Duc de Choiseul ensured that, for the first time, more money was spent on the navy than the army. Not only were fine new ships built, such as the splendid 110-gun *Ville de Paris,* but her officers were scientifically trained in tactics and among the admirals—D'Estaing,

place in those seas, none of which were decisive, chiefly because of faulty English signalling. Whereas their opponents had devised a system of flags denoting numbers which gave the commander-in-chief more flexibility in his orders, the English still fought with one hand tied behind their backs by the limited number of the old Fighting Instructions. Thus Rodney had a chance of victory at Martinique, but when he signalled his captains to engage their opposite ships in the French line, some of them imagined he meant the ship they ought to be opposite if the lines of battle were conterminous, whereas he actually meant the ship they found themselves opposite. More battles have been lost through bad signalling than from any other cause.

Admiral de Grasse
Admiral Sir Samuel Hood

The Battle of Chesapeake Bay

It was a fault of this kind which caused the most serious defeat of the war, though only one British ship was lost. This Battle of the Chesapeake (called by the Americans the battle of the Virginian Capes because it was fought between Cape Henry and Cape Charles at the ten-mile wide mouth of Chesapeake Bay) secured the independence of the United States. It was one of the decisive battles of the world, however half-hearted the actual engagement.

Briefly, the situation on land was that one British army was at New York and another, under General Cornwallis, was besieged at Yorktown, having failed to defeat Washington's army in the state of Virginia during the summer of 1781. Cornwallis's only chance of escape was the arrival of the British fleet, whereas Washington's only chance to defeat him was the arrival of troops and ships from France.

Two views of the Battle of the Chesapeake, French left, British right

Chesapeake, where another French fleet from the north joined him, making his total thirty-six ships of the line.

Only five days before his arrival, Admiral Sir Samuel Hood had passed the entrance of the bay on his way north to New York. Lord Rodney, the commander-in-chief in the West Indies, had expected some such development, and since he was himself on his way home because of ill-health he sent Hood up to New York to join Admiral Thomas Graves there. Their combined fleet amounted to only nineteen ships, but as there was no news of De Grasse they sailed south to relieve General Cornwallis.

When he arrived off Cape Henry on 5th September, Graves was astonished to see a large fleet straggling out to sea from the Chesapeake. It was a wonderful chance to engage before the enemy had formed line of battle. But Graves was not an intelligent admiral. Brought up in the tradition that a fleet should never engage before line of battle had been formed, he hoisted the signal for Line Ahead. Not only did this give De Grasse time to form his own line, but when it was hauled down and replaced by the signal to engage, Hood in the rear was confused. It was all very well for Admiral Samuel Drake in the van, who was close enough to engage the French van, but Hood was still far out of range because the opposing lines were not yet parallel.

A short action followed. Drake's rigging was cut up. Half of Grave's division in the centre got within range; the other half and all Hood's ships in the rear could not fire a shot. When darkness fell, the action was broken off. Next morning Graves called a conference of his officers, Hood, who had not been engaged

Cornwallis had about 7,000 men behind the fortifications of York-town, whereas Washington and Rochambeau were marching down the Chesapeake river with 8,000, and Layfayette with 4,500 French troops and American militia was at Williamsburg nearby. Everything depended on which fleet would sway the balance.

The Comte de Grasse, with a fleet of twenty-eight ships and 3,500 fresh troops, had recently arrived in the West Indies when he received Washington's appeal for help. On August 30th he arrived in the

was all for sailing into the bay. Drake, whose ships were badly damaged, objected. De Grasse, of course, expected another attack. But after the two fleets had lain in sight of each other for two days, Graves decided to retire to New York and leave Cornwallis to his fate. On 19th October the British army surrendered at Yorktown. Washington's armies and De Grasse's fleet had ensured the independence of the United States.

Rodney breaks the line

The war between Britain and her other enemies continued until 1783. The American colonies might be lost, but Canada, India and her other possessions would be safe provided she did not suffer another defeat at sea. Fortunately for her, in 1782, after peace negotiations had begun in Paris, Rodney won a resounding victory over De Grasse at the Battle of the Saintes, a passage between the islands of Dominica and Guadaloupe. Not

only did the success come at the right moment for Britain to demand better peace terms, but it also marked a revolution in tactics under sail. For the first time in a hundred years what began as a formal battle between two fleets sailing on opposite tacks turned, by the accident of a shift in the wind, into one in which the French line was broken in two places. Once a line of battle was broken, enemy ships could be raked or surrounded, and defeat was inevitable.

De Grasse with a fleet of thirty-three ships was escorting a large convoy intended for the invasion of Jamaica. Rodney, with Hood and Drake commanding the rear and van respectively, chased him with a fleet of thirty-six ships and damaged two of his ships slightly. De Grasse turned to prevent them falling into enemy hands, thus enabling Rodney to catch up with the main body on 12th April. Having lost the race for the weather gauge, he began to pass the French fleet on the opposite tack.

Battle of the Saintes

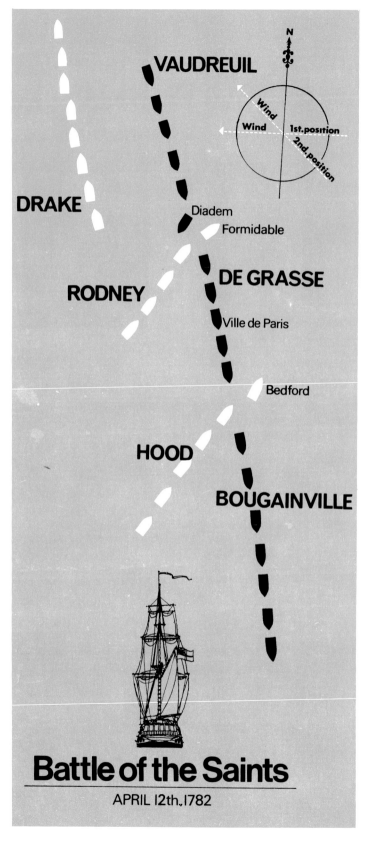

Battle of the Saints

APRIL 12th, 1782

The usual cannonade had begun when his flag captain, Sir Charles Douglas, a gunnery expert, peering through the smoke of battle saw a gap in the French line just astern of their flagship. It had been caused by a shift in the wind from east to south-east. The English sails now filled, but the French *Diadem* was taken aback, that is to say, her sails were flattened against the mast, her speed was checked and she slewed round, thereby creating a dangerous gap in the close-hauled line of battle formation of the rest of the fleet. The same thing happened to a ship in the van division.

Douglas begged the gouty old admiral, who was sitting in a chair on the quarterdeck, to steer through the gap. "Break the line, Sir George, and the day is ours and I will insure you the victory." "No," replied Rodney, "I will not break my line," thinking that Douglas referred to his own line. Then, as he awoke to the opportunity before him, he reluctantly agreed: "Well, well, do as you please." As his *Formidable* passed through the French line, her hundred guns raked the ships on either side. Six ships followed her, cutting off the French rear from their centre.

Meanwhile De Grasse in the huge *Ville de Paris* had forged ahead to follow the van division under Bougainville, the famous circumnavigator and the predecessor of Cook in the Pacific. More by chance than intention, Captain Affleck in the *Bedford* broke through a second gap, which developed between the two. All the ships in Hood's division followed him through. De Grasse was surrounded. After the *Ville de Paris* had been reduced to a wreck she struck the white flag of Bourbon France. She was the first three-decker in the war to surrender; nor had a commander-in-chief ever been

COUNT DE GRASSE *delivering his Sword to the Gallant* ADMIRAL RODNEY.

taken prisoner on board his own flagship.

Bougainville's ships escaped (Hood said because Rodney was too lazy to follow them), but De Grasse had lost ten altogether and the casualties on board his ship alone were greater than those of the whole British fleet. In all, 14,000 Frenchmen were killed or taken prisoner.

The victory did Rodney little good personally, because the first news he heard from England was that a new government had ordered him home so that he could be replaced by an admiral of a more favourable political complexion. To the embarrassment of the government, the news of his great victory arrived too late for a change of mind. But Rodney had set the example of breaking the line, thereby shattering the paralysing traditions of the old formal tactics. With the adoption of a new signal book based on French models, the new tactics were to bear

wonderful fruit in Nelson's generation. The old empire was lost because command of the sea was lost. A new one was to result from the discoveries of Captain Cook and by victories over a France made bankrupt and forced into revolution by the part she played in the war of American Independence.

Cartoon of surrender of De Grasse to Lord Rodney

Louis de Bougainville

CHAPTER 8

ST VINCENT AND CAMPERDOWN

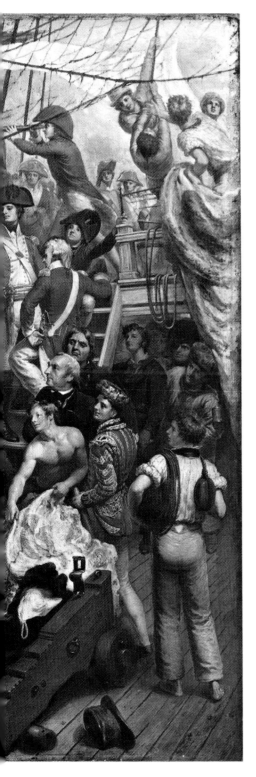

The year 1797 opened with a blizzard. The French fleet found itself in a snowstorm at Bantry Bay on the south-western coast of Ireland, where it was hoped to land troops under General Hoche and the Irish patriot Wolfe Tone to assist a rebellion against England. But the weather was so bad that not a man was landed, nor a shot fired. The only satisfaction on their return to Brest was that not a single British ship had been seen going out or coming home.

It was, indeed, the worst period for Britain during her twenty-year long war with revolutionary and Napoleonic France. Since war had been declared five years before, only one success had been won—Howe's victory over the Brest fleet on the Glorious First of June, 1794. The enemies of the French Revolution were being defeated at all points by armies which overwhelmed everything before them like a torrent. Holland was now the Batavian Republic, her fleet having been captured by cavalry over the ice! Austrian armies were defeated on the Rhine and in northern Italy, where a Cisalpine Republic was proclaimed. Every attempt of the British to land troops in Europe had been repulsed with ignominy, and the Italian victories of a young general named Napoleon Bonaparte, together with the formation

De Winter surrendering to Admiral Duncan

of a Franco-Spanish alliance, made the Mediterranean untenable by her fleet.

A plan for invasion

Encouraged by such military successes, an invasion of England was considered by the French government. The use of the Spanish and Dutch fleets in conjunction with that at Brest was planned. But the handling of fleets is not as easy as that of armies drunk with revolutionary enthusiasm. Early in 1797 the Spaniards were defeated off Cape St Vincent. In the autumn the Dutch were destroyed at Camperdown. In between, the seamen of the Royal Navy mutinied for two months. The paradox of the story of the stirring events of that year is that the one opportunity to invade England while her fleet lay paralysed was missed.

The stage is set

The Spanish fleet was under the command of Juan de Cordova, whose flagship, the *Santissima Trinidada,* was the largest warship afloat, a four-decker mounting 136 guns. As Nelson said when he met her at this battle and again at Trafalgar, the three-decker *Victory* of 100 guns was nothing to her. In addition, Cordova had six three-deckers and twenty two-deckers. It was suggested that he should come round from Cartagena to Cadiz and thence to Brest. The Spanish government agreed, because the move provided an opportunity of convoying four ships loaded with mercury from the mines at Malaga, an essential mineral for amalgamation with the silver brought from the New World. The safe passage of these valuable vessels was the only successful part of Cordova's voyage.

top: *Model of* H.M.S. Boyne *1790*

middle: *Section of 74-gun ship (two-decker)*

This was because Sir John Jervis, with fifteen ships of the line (only three of them three-deckers), was waiting for him off Cape St Vincent. This cape, a hundred miles southeast of Trafalgar, is the most westerly point of the continent of Europe. From time immemorial mariners have saluted the headland by lowering their topsails. From his palace at Sagres on this cape Prince Henry the Navigator had watched the sails of his explorer's caravels disappear below the horizon on their way to discover the unknown coast-line of Africa. Ever since, on account of its strategic position between the Straits of Gibraltar and the Atlantic ports, dozens of battles have been fought in its vicinity.

In size and fire power the Spanish fleet was twice as strong as the British, but not in seamanship and efficiency. Horatio Nelson, an obscure captain aged thirty-eight, expressed his opinion that "of all the fleets I ever saw, I never saw one in point of officers and men equal to our present one, and with a commander-in-chief fit to lead them to glory."

Jervis (created Earl St Vincent after his victory) deserves the tribute. Aged sixty-two, he had devoted the whole of his life to the naval service. The command of this fleet gave him the opportunity of using his formidable talents for training a fleet

bottom: *Bone model of French 120-gun ship made by prisoners-of-war*

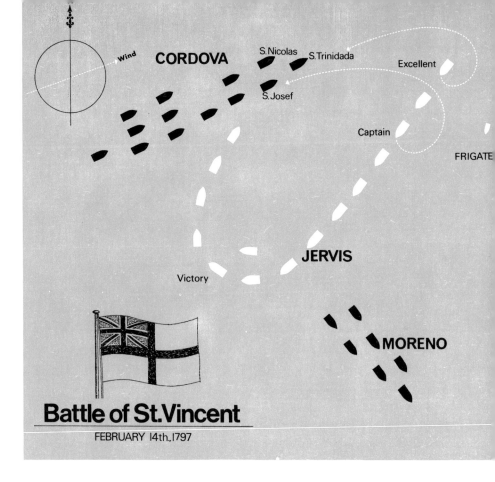

Battle of St.Vincent

FEBRUARY 14th., 1797

for battle. It was part of the same fleet which Nelson was to lead to victory at the Nile the following year, when he told his old master that "we look to you as our father, under whose fostering care we have been led to fame."

The band of brothers

He was speaking for all his "band of brothers" (as he called his fellow captains) whom Jervis had trained. He himself had just been promoted to a bigger ship, the *Captain* (seventy-four guns), because Jervis had discerned his promise. There was Thomas Troubridge leading the line in the *Culloden,* to whom Jervis paid a noble tribute when he spoke of "his honour and courage bright as his sword." There was Nelson's old friend Cuthbert Collingwood as captain of the *Excellent,* the rear ship of the line. There was Thomas

Foley, who was to lead the fleet at the Nile, and Ben Hallowell, both giants of men. When on February 14th, 1797, the Spanish fleet was encountered, "Old Oak" (as the king called Jervis) knew that he could trust his captains, so he attacked a fleet twice his size because, as he said, "a victory is essential to England at this moment."

Into battle

As the thick mist lifted on that morning of St. Valentine's Day the strength of the enemy was gradually revealed. "There are eight of the line, Sir John," reported his flag captain.

"Very well, sir."

"There are twenty-five of the line, Sir John."

"Very well, sir."

"There are twenty-seven sail, Sir John."

"Enough, sir, no more of that: the die is cast, and if there are fifty sail I will go through them."

"That's right, Sir John," exclaimed the gigantic Hallowell, slapping the admiral on the back in his excitement, "that's right, by God we shall give them a damned good licking."

The Spaniards were sailing in two groups, the foremost under Vice-Admiral Moreno, included the mercury vessels (which escaped the battle altogether); the rear and larger group was under Cordova. Jervis steered a course to divide the two and concentrate on the rearmost. When the British line in close line ahead formation was between them, Cordova altered course in order to pass astern. Maintaining the order of his line, Jervis signalled his ships to tack in succession in order to follow him round. As the leading ship, *Culloden*, came round it was obvious to Nelson, whose *Captain* lay third from the rear, that by the time the whole line had turned Cordova would have achieved his aim because he had the advantage of the wind. At one o'clock he therefore took his ship out of the line on his own initiative in order to anticipate the Spanish move.

The genius of Nelson

By throwing his two-decker across the path of the four-decker *Santissima Trinidada,* which was supported by three three-deckers astern of her, Nelson forced them to alter course, thereby giving Jervis's ships time to work their way into the main body. Only a tactician of genius, confident of his own judgment and utterly without fear, would have dared to do this, because it was done without orders and also might well have resulted in

the destruction of his smaller ship.

It was in this way that an obscure officer sailed into history. Had he failed, he would have been court-martialled and the world might never have heard of him. As it was, he engaged the towering *Santissima Trinidada* as she sailed past him, and then attacked the *San Josef* of 112 guns and the *San Nicolas* of eighty, which were sailing in her wake. The *Culloden* was already on the spot, while Collingwood brought the *Excellent* from the other end of the line to support his friend, again without orders.

Nelson took his ship alongside the *San Josef*, gave her a terrific broadside and then boarded her, himself leading his men over the side. Having cleared her upper deck in hand to hand fighting, he found that her rigging was entangled with that of the *San Nicolas* on the other side. "I directed my people to board the first-rate, which was done in an instant. A Spanish officer looked over the quarterdeck rail and said they surrendered; from this most welcome intelligence it

Nelson boarding the San Josef

Admiral Lord Duncan

mutiny in the history of the Royal Navy which paralysed the fleet in the middle of a war should have taken place two months after this battle. But it must be remembered that the mutiny only affected the fleets stationed at Portsmouth, the mouth of the Thames and the North Sea; it never spread to the Mediterranean because Jervis's iron discipline checked it at the outset.

This is not the place to describe that extraordinary episode. Suffice it to say that it was a justifiable strike against low wages (which had not been altered since the days of Oliver Cromwell), bad food and intolerable conditions on board. It was conducted with remarkable restraint by the mutineers, and most of their demands were met. But when it spread to the North Sea fleet at Yarmouth it meant that Admiral Duncan and Vice-Admiral Onslow had to conduct the blockade of the Dutch fleet in the Texel with their two loyal ships only, signalling to an imaginary fleet over the horizon in order to prevent the enemy knowing what was happening.

Adam Duncan, tall, grey-haired, with great physical strength even at the age of sixty-six, quelled a mutiny on board his own ship by holding a rebel over the side with one hand and threatening to drop him into the sea if he did not desist. This amiable Scots giant had been in command of the North Sea fleet for the past two years. His ships were the worst in the navy, even his flagship, the *Venerable,* being so leaky that she could not stay at sea for long at a time. His duty was to watch the Dutch fleet, now in revolutionary hands. At times he was assisted by a Russian squadron, which was fortunately absent on the day of battle because it caused him more trouble than it was worth.

was not long before I was on the quarterdeck, where the Spanish captain, with a bow, presented me his sword, and said the admiral was dying of his wounds below." Such was what came to be called Nelson's Patent Bridge for Boarding First-Rates.

His own ship was "dreadfully mauled" and had run out of ammunition, having expended 146 barrels of powder. She was in no condition to continue the fight, nor could other British ships pursue the Spanish remnant which reached Cadiz. Jervis took his own ships to Gibraltar, together with four large prizes. He had made certain that no Spanish fleet would assist the French plan for invasion.

Mutiny!

It may seem odd that the only

Under sailing orders

The Dutch were commanded by Jan Willem de Winter, a much younger man who had been a soldier though he was brought up to the sea. He was as big as Duncan, who remarked after the battle that it was surprising that two such gigantic objects should have escaped unscathed. De Winter sympathized with the aims of the French Revolution and renamed his ships in suitable revolutionary style, his flagship being called *Vrijheid* (Liberty). In all, he had sixteen ships of the line and five frigates, and a fine record of Dutch victories at sea to sustain him.

Unfortunately for him, his political masters had little idea of naval warfare. During the summer there was much talk of another invasion by Hoche and Wolfe Tone. But now Hoche was dead and Wolfe Tone abandoned in Paris, and the plan was dropped. The naval committee at the Hague, however, felt that for prestige reasons their fleet should go to sea and offer battle. Unwillingly, De Winter did so on 7th October.

The Battle of Camperdown

His appearance was at once signalled to Duncan at Yarmouth by the inshore squadron watching the mouth of the Texel. De Winter had only progressed forty miles along the Dutch coast when he was told that Duncan had put to sea in pursuit. Doubting the capabilities of his own ships, he turned for home, and in so doing laid a trap for the English by stealing along the coast in shallow water, his ships being of shallower draft than those of the English. He might be able to lure Duncan on to a lee shore where the possibilities of shipwreck were great.

But he overlooked two things: the high standard of seamanship that a fleet which had been constantly at sea was bound to achieve; and the excellence of British gunnery, which enabled them to fire three rounds to the enemy's one, in addition to possessing eighty-six carronades, a new and powerful short range weapon. The Dutch may have had the advantage in numbers and position: the British were better trained and determined to erase the shameful record of the

Battle of Camperdown, Dutch on left

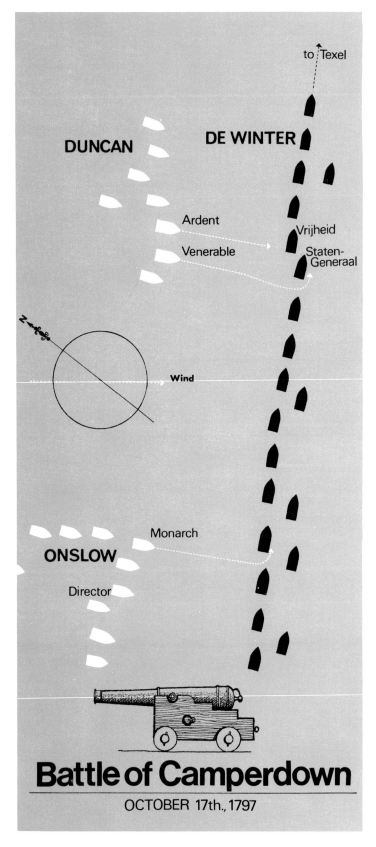

DUNCAN

DE WINTER

to Texel

Ardent

Vrijheid

Venerable

Staten-Generaal

Wind

Monarch

ONSLOW

Director

Battle of Camperdown
OCTOBER 17th., 1797

late mutinies. Thus the battle off Camperdown on 17th October, 1797, was the hardest fought in the long war at sea, and the casualties were higher in proportion.

Camperdown is a village fifteen miles from the Texel. As Duncan approached the coast under full sail in order to cut off De Winter's retreat, it is said that he told his men to keep up a good fire because there was a hard winter coming. Another story is that when he saw a thirteen-year old midshipman duck his head when the ships opened fire, he patted the boy on the back, saying "Very well, my boy, but don't do it again. You might put your head in the way of a shot." Again, when his pilot complained that they might run on shore (the battle was viewed by spectators on the beach only a mile away), Duncan replied "Go on at your peril, for I am determined to fight the ships on land if I cannot by sea."

The tactics he employed have some similarity to those later seen at Trafalgar. But whereas Nelson approached the enemy in two well organized columns, Duncan did so in two loose groups. Such was his anxiety to intercept De Winter that he did not have time to formulate a plan of action. He hoped to break the line at all points, as Howe had tried to do in 1794, but in the event his approach was so hasty that his captains did pretty much as they wanted. As one Scotsman complained, throwing down his signal book in disgust, "Damn me! Up wi' the hel-lm and gang into the middle o' it!"

Thus the British fleet was in no sort of order beyond two ill-defined groups, one headed by Onslow in the *Monarch,* the other by Duncan in the *Venerable.* Nor can any connected account be given of the mêlée which developed when they swept down upon the enemy's line. Duncan aimed at getting between the *Vrijheid* and the *Staten-Generaal* in the centre of the line, but the latter closed up so quickly that he had to go astern of her and was in danger of being surrounded by other Dutch ships. The *Ardent* of only sixty-four guns bore the brunt of De Winter's fire, her captain being killed within ten minutes of the start.

For two hours the *Vrijheid* and the *Venerable* were the centre of a dog-fight between half a dozen ships. By half past two in the afternoon De Winter was the only unwounded officer on board the former. Action had ceased in the rear, where Onslow had overwhelmed his opponents. With his own hands De Winter was trying to hoist a signal when the halliards were shot away by a new entrant into the dog-fight—the *Director,* under Captain William Bligh of *Bounty* fame. He belonged to Onslow's squadron, but had fought his way up the Dutch line in time to give the *coup de grâce* to their flagship.

Duncan told him to bring De Winter on board the *Venerable,* which was too badly damaged to move. Bligh sent a lieutenant on board, where he found De Winter trying to escape in the ship's boat. He surrendered and, "taking leave of a young officer, his nephew, who was desperately wounded, accompanied me to the gangway, the officers and men making way for him, and many kneeling to take leave of their beloved commander."

When De Winter reached Duncan's quarterdeck he proffered his sword. Duncan refused it with the words: "I would much rather take a brave man's hand than his sword." Not surprisingly, the two men became firm friends. Their battle was the last, and the fiercest, of the many fought between two nations who lived by the sea, and who prided themselves on their prowess as fighters under sail.

Battle of Camperdown; capture of the Vrijheid

CHAPTER 9

THE NILE AND TRAFALGAR

Alexander the Great conquered the known world before he was thirty. Napoleon Bonaparte, aged twenty-nine, thought he might do something of the same sort after his brilliant Italian campaign. The French government encouraged his ambition, because it was dangerous, in those revolutionary days, to have a successful military genius at home. Plans for an expedition to Egypt, with vague prospects of an advance towards India, gained easy acceptance. Tippoo Sahib, Sultan of Mysore, who had been at war with the British for many years, was sent the token of a tricolour to stick in his turban; but that was all the assistance he ever received.

The struggle between France and Britain was fundamentally one between land power, personified by Napoleon, and sea power, of which Nelson was the embodiment. The first stage of the conflict was the Egyptian Expedition of 1798. Napoleon conquered Egypt; but after Nelson's victory at the Nile his army was left to wither in the desert like cut flowers in a vase, because all communications with France were severed when her fleet was destroyed in Aboukir Bay.

Imperial ambitions

The force intended for the expedition which assembled at Toulon that spring was very impressive: 30,000 infantry, 3,000 cavalry, 300 transport vessels escorted by a battle fleet of thirteen ships of the line and seven frigates, under the command of Admiral Brueys. Bonaparte (as he then called himself) had with him many of the future marshals of France, whose names were to be renowned throughout Europe in the years to come—Berthier, Murat, Marmont. Nor was it to be merely a military conquest: it was to include the rediscovery of the lost civilization of ancient Egypt. It was one of the glories of the expedition that the group of *savants* who sailed with it founded the science of Egyptology. Unfortunately for them, most of their discoveries, such as the Rosetta Stone, are now in the British Museum, not the Louvre. Such was one of the remoter consequences of the Battle of the Nile.

The expedition sailed on 10th May, 1798. Making directly for Malta, Bonaparte had only to knock on the gates of the ancient citadel for the Knights of St John to surrender. As he remarked after viewing the fortifications which had withstood so many Turkish sieges, it was fortunate there was someone to open the gates. Having taken possession of the island by treachery, dissolved the Order and looted its treasure, within a week he sailed on to Alexandria.

Admiral Lord Nelson, portrait by Abbott

On his arrival there on 1st June he was surprised to learn that Nelson had been there the day before in search of him. He was not alarmed, for he never understood the implications of sea power. It was sufficient that he had arrived. Brueys was left with the fleet in Aboukir Bay. The army disembarked, marched across the desert, captured and defeated the Mamelukes at the Battle of the Pyramids, all within a month. Such was to be the pattern of Napoleonic campaigns for the next ten years.

Meanwhile Nelson had been chasing around the Mediterranean in a vain endeavour to find the French. Ten years older than Bonaparte, he was now a frail, energetic, battered little man, who had lost his right arm and the sight of his right eye. We have seen how he made his reputation the previous year at the Battle of St Vincent, when the British fleet was still excluded from the Mediterranean.

A brave little fleet

Early in 1798 it was decided to send a small fleet into that sea again, the main body remaining off Cadiz under Earl St Vincent. He it was who recommended that Nelson should lead it. It was a small, select fleet of fourteen two-deckers, together with one ship of only fifty guns, and a few frigates. It could not compare in fire-power with the French, who had three ships of over eighty guns and the huge *L'Orient* of 120 guns as flagship, the largest three-decker afloat. But Nelson's Band of Brothers were of the same calibre as Bonaparte's marshals, and the easy, intimate terms on which he was with them provide a model in the art of leadership. Meeting and talking with the admiral on frequent occasions,

every possible manœuvre was discussed, so that when the moment for action came a few signals sufficed to give them the chance to show their initiative. Every captain knew exactly what was required of him.

Looking for action

Unfortunately, while sheltering off Sardinia, Nelson lost touch with his frigates, the eyes of the fleet, as he

called them. They never rejoined, a
fact which explains the long chase
around the eastern Mediterranean.
It was not until he took the fleet to
Naples that he learned that the
French had been seen heading
south-east. By intuition rather than
information he guessed their
destination was Alexandria. "You
may be assured I will fight them the
moment I can reach them, be they
at anchor or under sail," he told
St Vincent, and the chase began.

He reached Alexandria two days
before Bonaparte, the fleets having
passed each other in the night. The
watchers on the minarets could
almost see his ship departing eastward while the French appeared
from the west. Finding the harbour
empty, Nelson hastened on towards
the Levant, striving to pick up news
where the French might be found.
He had no luck. In a despairing
mood, he circled back to Sicily,
where for the first time he was

*Battle of the Nile,
French fleet in
foreground*

Admiral Brueys

accurately informed of their destination.

Under press of sail, he was back again at Alexandria on the morning of August 1st. A mass of shipping lay there, but where was the battle fleet? Little was known about that coast. Captain Foley of the *Goliath* had an old atlas which marked a few soundings in the bay of Aboukir, fifteen miles east of Alexandria. Other captains regarded the map as useless for navigation, but it was enough for Foley and for Nelson.

The Battle of Aboukir Bay

By the afternoon the fleet had reached the castle on Aboukir point. A boy at the masthead of the leading ship, *Zealous*, suddenly saw a line of French ships lying at anchor across the bay. He slid down a rope to tell his captain for fear that the enemy might hear him if he shouted. By the time he reached the deck the other leading ship, *Goliath*,

had already signalled that the enemy was in sight.

Brueys fancied himself secure in this broad anchorage. He had just received the news of the Battle of the Pyramids and was preparing to celebrate Bonaparte's birthday. For several weeks his ships had been lying there, anchored 500 feet apart, in a long line across the bay, with four frigates safely inside the line. All would have been well if his van ship had anchored closer to the shoal water off Aboukir point, and had the other ships been closer together. But it was now late in the afternoon with only two hours' daylight left. The English had no pilots and no charts. There was no need to man the guns on the landward sides of his ships. The enemy were in no sort of formation as they streamed round the point. A battle seemed out of the question, though Brueys might have recalled what happened at Quiberon Bay.

It was now that Nelson reaped the reward of all those discussions

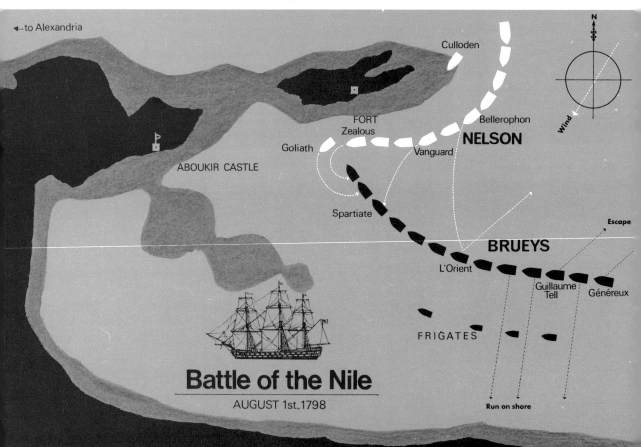

<-- to Alexandria

Culloden

N

FORT
Zealous
Bellerophon

Goliath
Vanguard
NELSON

ABOUKIR CASTLE

Wind

Spartiate

Escape

BRUEYS

L'Orient

Guillaume
Tell
Généreux

FRIGATES

Battle of the Nile

AUGUST 1st, 1798

Run on shore

Loss of L'Orient

with his captains. The wind was blowing directly along the French line. Only three signals were required: Prepare for battle. Concentrate on the enemy's van and centre. Anchor by the stern as soon as a ship fetches up opposite one of the enemy. Foley took the hint and the *Goliath*, closely followed by the *Zealous* (Captain Samuel Hood), squeezed in between the five fathom shoal line and the first of the French ships. They were inside the enemy line, on the side on which the guns had not been manned. Five ships followed them round, each anchoring ahead of the last. The British seamen were at their stations, stripped to the waist, with black handkerchiefs round their heads. The guns were run out of the ports. The customary three cheers echoed across the waters of the bay as each successive ship took up her station.

Nelson in the *Vanguard* had dropped back to be in the centre of the line that was forming as the ships entered the bay. With five already engaging the enemy from the landward side, he led the remaining ships to engage on the seaward side. All except one—the unfortunate *Culloden,* which had lagged behind the main body and in her haste to catch up, cut the corner of the shoal off Aboukir island too sharply. She went aground and did not get off until all was over.

As the *Vanguard* brought to opposite the *Spartiate* she came under heavy fire, for the French fought with desperate valour. The *Guerrière* for instance, was dismasted within ten minutes, but she refused to surrender until three hours later, in spite of repeated calls to do so. The fire from the *Spartiate* was so hot that Nelson himself was wounded by a splinter, a deep wound on his forehead. Blinded with blood and suffering from concussion, he was taken

Nelson's wound being dressed in cockpit

down to the surgeon in the cockpit crying, "I am killed! Remember me to my wife!"

But the rest of his ships had passed ahead of him. It was the *Bellerophon* (called by her men the "Billy Ruff'n") which first engaged the flagship *L'Orient,* lying seventh in the line, a seventy-four two-decker against a 120-gun three-decker. For an hour she fought it out, until, after suffering 200 casualties, she was driven off and drifted away to seaward.

Some idea of the ferocity of the fighting as darkness fell is given by a gunner who asked a powder-monkey sitting on a chest of ammunition to hand him another cartridge. The boy did not move. The gunner pushed him and he fell stiffly on to the deck. He had been killed by the blast. Another lad, "who had a match in his hand to fire his gun, was in the act of applying it when a shot took off his arm. It hung by a small piece of skin and the match fell to the deck. He looked at his arm and seeing what had happened, seized the match in his left hand and fired the gun before he went to the cockpit to have it dressed."

L'Orient had fought off the initial attacks, but other ships were now concentrating their fire on her, converging like mastiffs on a wounded bull. Flames broke out from her stern. Her admiral had both legs shot off, but with a tourniquet strapped to each stump Brueys sat in a chair directing operations until a cannon ball killed him by nearly cutting him in two. His flag captain, Casabianca (whose son had lost a leg) continued to fight the ship, an incident later made famous in a popular ballad, *The Boy Stood on the Burning Deck.* Others threw themselves overboard to swim to safety, since it was now obvious that the ship would soon blow up when the fire reached the magazine. At ten o'clock, under what an eye witness called "the cold, placid light of the moon", the French flagship exploded with such force that awestruck spectators paused at their guns to contemplate such a tremendous catastrophe. The sound and the sudden flash in the sky was seen as far away as Alexandria. When she went down she took with her half a million pounds in bullion and three tons of plate looted at Malta.

Nelson was brought on deck to witness the final agony, but weakness from loss of blood compelled him to retire before the actual explosion. For another hour French ships in the rear continued to fire, but when the *Franklin* surrendered all was over and exhausted men sank to sleep, beside their guns.

Aftermath

The scene at dawn after eleven ships had been taken or driven on shore was thus described: "I went on deck to view the state of the fleets, and an awful sight it was. The whole bay was covered with dead bodies, mangled, wounded and scorched, not a bit of clothes on them except their trousers." Only two French line-of-battle ships escaped the jaws of Nelson's crocodile: the *Généreux* and the *Guillaume Tell,* commanded by Villeneuve, whom we shall meet again at Trafalgar. Both ships were later captured.

Nelson's account of the battle in a letter to Lord Howe, victor of the Glorious First of June in 1794, gives full credit to his captains: "I

L'Orient *exploding at night*

Prayers after the Battle of the Nile

had the happiness to command a band of brothers. Each knew his duty, and I was sure each would feel for a French ship. By attacking the enemy's van and centre, the wind blowing directly along their line, I was enabled to throw what force I pleased on a few ships. This plan my friends readily conceived by the signals for which we are principally indebted to your lordship. . . . Had it not pleased God that I had been wounded stone blind, there cannot be a doubt but that every ship would have been in our possession."

"The glorious victory," wrote the British ambassador at Naples, "is like the church of St. Peter's at Rome. It strikes at first sight from its majesty, but the more you examine its dimensions and details the more wonderful it appears." Not only was it the most complete naval victory on record in its destruction of an entire fleet, but its

political consequences were equally striking. The French lost 9,000 men killed or taken prisoner, apart from the fact that Bonaparte's army was left marooned in Egypt. British casualties numbered 895. The brilliant and spontaneous way in which the battle was fought astounded Europe. Whereas at the beginning of the year Britain dared not enter the Mediterranean for lack of allies, now the Austrian, Russian and Turkish empires joined her against France. Minorca and Malta soon fell into her hands as invaluable bases for her fleet. Lord Nelson (as he now became) passed through central Europe on his way home as a conquering hero. At Vienna, Haydn even composed a Mass in his honour. The journey was the more extraordinary because he was accompanied by Emma, Lady Hamilton, the wife of the ambassador at Naples, and one of the world's most famous romances had begun.

What of Bonaparte? After an attempt to fight his way back via Constantinople had been foiled at Acre again by sea power, he left his army in the lurch and slipped back home in a frigate commanded by Ganteaume, of whom (like Villeneuve) we shall read again in the year of Trafalgar. This was a year after the destruction of his fleet. His army was left to rot in the desert until it was defeated by an amphibious expedition under the command of Admiral Keith and General Abercromby in 1801. On that occasion the flagship struck the submerged wreck of *L'Orient*. Part of her mainmast was retrieved and shaped into a coffin in which Nelson's body was placed in 1805. In 1801 he was not in the Mediterranean: he was in the Baltic, winning fresh laurels by defeating the Danes at the Battle of Copenhagen.

Britain at bay

In September, 1805, a month before the battle of Trafalgar, Nelson was shown into a room in London where he met a general whose face he did not recognize. Since Sir Arthur Wellesley (later the Duke of Wellington) had spent most of his career in India, this was not surprising. Nelson, on the other hand, was the most idolized man in England. His series of brilliant victories, his personality and appearance, one armed and one eyed, made him the sort of war hero every people demands. Vanity, however, was one of his less attractive characteristics. He tried to impress this unknown general by entering "into conversation with me, if I can call it conversation, for it was all on his side and all about himself, and in a style so vain and so silly as to

disgust me." Realizing that he was not making a good impression, Nelson left the room to find out who he was talking to. He returned, says Wellington, "to talk like an officer and a statesman. He was really a very superior man."

Such was the man who was killed at the height of his fame in the most decisive battle in British naval history. It was his death, not his victory, which most impressed people at that time, because it came at a critical point in the long war with France. For three years past, Britain had stood in fear of invasion from Boulogne. Had the Emperor, as Napoleon now called himself, been able to cross the "ditch", as he considered the Channel, in the eight hours which he fondly hoped would be sufficient, he might well have become master of the world. The British army was a poor thing compared with the 100,000 men of the Grand Army who were shortly to conquer Europe. Everything depended on the blockade of the French ports, a task involving almost the whole force of the Royal Navy, which at that date consisted of eighty-eight ships of the line, 125 frigates and some 140,000 seamen. Watching Boulogne itself there was a squadron under Keith. Off Brest lay the main Channel fleet under Cornwallis, closely blockading Ganteaume's twenty-one big ships. Off Cadiz a watch was kept on the Spanish fleet, then in alliance with France, while off Toulon Nelson commanded the Mediterranean fleet guarding Villeneuve's eleven ships.

Nelson preferred the method of open blockade, consisting of cruises off Toulon in the hope that the enemy would come out and fight. It was not so exhausting, nor so effective a method as the close blockade of Brest by Cornwallis, and when Villeneuve did come out

H.M.S. Victory

in March, 1805, Nelson missed him.

During the first part of the Trafalgar campaign Napoleon's grand strategy nearly succeeded. This was a well conceived diversionary scheme by which the Toulon and Cadiz fleets would unite and escape to the West Indies, where they would be joined by Ganteaume from Brest. Then the combined fleets would return to overwhelm Cornwallis and sail up the Channel to protect the crossing of 2,000 boats and transports of the Grand Army. It was the plan of the Spanish Armada on a much grander scale.

Villeneuve escaped from Toulon. He picked up the Cadiz fleet and they reached Martinique. But after waiting some weeks, Ganteaume failed to appear. Villeneuve therefore took the Franco-Spanish fleet back to Vigo, Corunna and Ferrol, brushing past a small British force off those ports at the end of July.

Nelson had no idea of this strategic plan. When he found that the French had gone from Toulon he sailed east, thinking it might be a repetition of the Egyptian Expedition. Then he thought better and sailed west, first hearing of the probable destination of the French from an officer in the Portuguese navy. He stretched across the Atlantic, again failed to locate the enemy, and returned disconsolate to Cadiz. Leaving some of his ships there under the command of Collingwood, and the rest with Cornwallis, he returned to Portsmouth in the *Victory*.

So far Napoleon had succeeded, though Ganteaume had failed to break the iron grip of Cornwallis which held him at Brest. The critical date of the campaign was August 12th, when Villeneuve emerged from Ferrol. Should he go north and challenge the augmented force of Cornwallis, or should he go south for the safety of Cadiz? He chose the latter course, in spite of frantic letters which he received from the Emperor to "lose not a minute, but enter the Channel with my united fleets. England is ours; we are quite ready and everything is embarked. Come only for twenty-four hours and all is over."

Napoleon drives east

Villeneuve was probably right, for the day after he wrote that letter—August 28th—Napoleon changed his mind. Austria was arming. His admirals had failed him. England was no longer the objective. The Grand Army broke camp and marched south to win the battle of Ulm the day after Trafalgar, to be followed by Austerlitz and the ensuing victories which took it to Moscow. Villeneuve was to be replaced by another admiral and the fleet would return to the Mediterranean. It was for that reason that Villeneuve (who did not stay for his successor) took the combined fleet out of Cadiz on 19th October, steering south for Gibraltar, not for England.

The Nelson Touch

On 13th September Nelson had left Portsmouth to take over the command of Collingwood's seventeen ships off Cadiz. One can imagine how determined he was that Villeneuve should not escape him again. He decided on a novel form of attack which would enable him, with his inferior numbers, to destroy the major part of the enemy by breaking their line in two places with two independent divisions, himself leading one and Collingwood the other.

"I think it will surprise and con-

found the enemy," he wrote, "They don't know what I am about. It will bring forward a pell-mell battle, and that is what I want." When he explained this "Nelson touch" to his captains it was "like an electric shock. It was new—it was singular—it was simple!" "It must succeed," they told him, and added "if ever they allow us to get at them! You are, my lord, surrounded by friends whom you inspire with confidence."

Such was the high state of morale on board the British ships as they lay over the horizon so that the enemy in Cadiz harbour should not know how many there were of them. Advanced frigates watched the slow emergence of the Franco-Spanish fleet from the bay on 19th October, watched it forming into line and steering south towards Gibraltar, and then off Cape Trafalgar watched it reverse course because Villeneuve did not trust his ships in a light wind against such an implacable adversary as Nelson. He hoped that he would regain the safety of Cadiz about ten miles away before it was too late.

It was a fatal move. His line was thrown into confusion because of the prevailing light airs, so that when, at dawn, on 21st October, Nelson's ships appeared in two columns from the west, Villeneuve's fleet was in an untidy crescent with several gaps in it.

The southern or leeward column led by Collingwood in the *Royal Sovereign* had been allotted the task of breaking the line and concentrating on the rear third of the enemy, each ship steering a course which would bring her opposite an enemy ship. According to the final injunction in Nelson's memorandum issued to all captains before the battle, "no captain can do very wrong if he places his ship alongside that of an enemy."

*Admiral
Lord Collingwood*

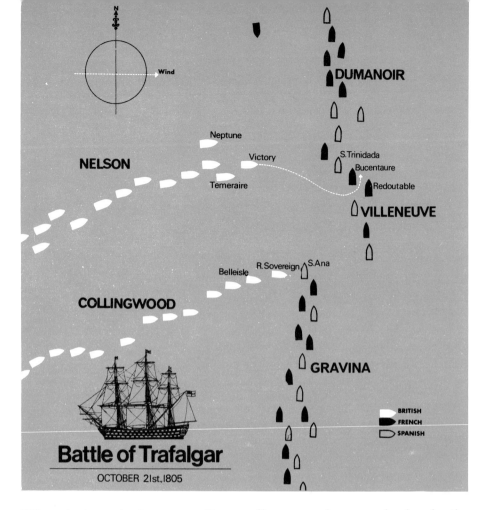

Battle of Trafalgar

OCTOBER 21st, 1805

"The glorious day's renown"

Nelson's northern or windward column was about a mile away from the enemy when Collingwood opened fire at noon. The rate of progress of both columns was incredibly slow as they bore down, owing to the absence of wind. Collingwood passed the time munching an apple. A description from the *Belleisle* astern of him (a British ship in spite of her name) gives a good impression of this tense approach to battle: "The silence on board was almost awful, broken only by the firm voice of the captain saying Steady! or Starboard a little! which was repeated by the master to the quartermaster at the helm, and occasionally by an officer calling to the impatient men, Lie down there, you, sir. As we got nearer and nearer to the enemy the silence was, however, broken by the shrieks of the wounded, for we had more than fifty of them before we fired a shot."

It was at this time that Nelson decided "to amuse the fleet with a signal," the famous Trafalgar signal, which was made in twelve hoists with numeral flags referring to words in a vocabulary; 253 (England) 269 (Expects) 863 (That) 261 (Every) 471 (Man) 958 (Will) 220 (Do) 370 (His) 4 (D) 21 (U) 19 (T) 24 (Y). Originally Nelson had suggested "England confides", but the last word was not in the vocabulary, so "Expects" was substituted; similarly "Duty" was not there, so the word had to be spelled out with flags referring to letters of the alphabet.

The admiral had an intuition that he would not survive the day. When the captain of a frigate bade him farewell with the words, "I trust on my return to find your lordship is in possession of twenty prizes," Nelson replied, "God bless you, Blackwood, I shall never see you again." He retired to his cabin, where he composed a prayer before going into action: "May the Great God whom I worship, grant to my Country, and for the benefit of Europe in general, a great and glorious victory; and may no misconduct in anyone, tarnish it; and may humanity after victory be the predominant feature in the British Fleet. For myself individually, I commit my life to Him who made me, and may His blessing light upon my endeavours for serving my Country faithfully. To Him I resign myself, and the just cause which is entrusted to me to defend. Amen, Amen. Amen."

His column was in an unusual formation. It might be compared to a heavily weighted spear, with three powerful ships at the head: *Victory* (100 guns), *Temeraire* (ninety-eight) and *Neptune* (ninety-eight). By all the rules of gunnery the *Victory's* perpendicular approach to the Spanish and French flagships, *Santissima Trinidada* (the four-decker he last saw at the battle of St Vincent) and *Bucentaure,* should have been fatal, because her course exposed her to the broadsides of the enemy while she could only reply with her bow guns. But Nelson was always one to take a calculated risk and he had a small opinion of enemy gunnery. Even so, her mizzen topmast and wheel were shot away before she engaged.

"It's warm work," he remarked to his flag captain, Masterman Hardy, as he paced the quarterdeck with all his decorations blazing on his uniform. Not until 12.25 did the *Victory's* treble-shotted guns speak.

Battle of Trafalgar, by Turner

vital point at which Nelson's spear struck, pushing aside the *Redoutable* and raking the decks of the *Bucentaure* with terrible effect. One by one the ships astern of the *Victory* came into action as the mêlée which he predicted developed as soon as the line was broken.

Death of a hero

Four ships were locked in deadly combat—*Bucentaure, Victory, Redoutable* and *Temeraire.* Captain Lucas of the *Redoutable* fought his ship with intrepid courage, though his French ship was only a two-decker surrounded by English three-deckers. At one point he almost boarded the *Victory,* but what he calls the "murderous" broadside from the British *Temeraire* killed two hundred of his men at one stroke. Half an hour after the struggle began, one of his marks-

The gundeck of the Victory today, with mess tables and hammocks

Nelson mortally wounded at Trafalgar

On her approach the enemy line closed up, the bows of the *Bucentaure* (80 guns) almost touching the towering stern of the *Santissima Trinidada* (130), while the bowsprit of the smaller *Redoutable* (74) touched the former's taffrail. This was the

The Death of Nelson, by Devis

Captain Masterman Hardy

men stationed in the tops shot Nelson at a range of only sixty feet, so close were the ships locked. A midshipman, who was standing by the admiral as he fell, fired in return and killed the man. Nelson was carried below. The bullet (which is preserved at Windsor Castle) entered his left shoulder and broke his spine. Down in the dark cockpit, illuminated by lanterns as the surgeons went about their bloody business, Nelson lay dying as the sounds of battle raged above him for the next four hours. The log of the ship concludes: "Partial firing continued until 4.30, when a victory having been reported to the Right Hon. Lord Nelson, he died of his wounds." His last words were "Kiss me, Hardy . . . Thank God I have done my duty."

Only four of the seventeen prizes taken on that memorable day were secured, because after the battle a

Seaman Brown

Nelson's coxwain Allen

storm blew up which wrecked most of the others. A few enemy ships, chiefly from the van under Dumanoir, reached Cadiz. The *Victory* had to be towed to Gibraltar because she was almost dismasted. But whereas the British killed numbered 429, those of the enemy killed or drowned were over 2,800.

Collingwood's despatch opens with the words, "Yesterday a battle was fought by His Majesty's fleet which will stand recorded as one of the most brilliant and decisive that ever distinguished the British navy. Our loss has been great in men, but what is irreparable and the cause of universal lamentation is the death of the noble commander-in-chief, who died in the arms of victory."

That was the feeling in London when the news reached the capital on November 7th, the bearer having ridden up from Falmouth in twenty-four hours. "I never saw so little public joy," wrote an observer, "Every common person in the streets speaking first of their sorrow for Nelson, and then of the victory." That is why, in the centre of Trafalgar Square, Nelson's statue stands at the top of the highest pillar in London, overlooking the Admiralty, while his tomb is in St Paul's Cathedral.

The British stranglehold

Just how decisive Nelson's last victory was only became clear as the years advanced. It did not save Britain from invasion, because Napoleon had already changed his plans. But the destruction of the main Franco-Spanish fleet compelled the Emperor to pit the conquest of Europe against Britain's mastery of the surrounding seas. Thus the war, which lasted ten years after Trafalgar, developed into an epic struggle between land and

sea power. Because Nelson's victories enabled the Royal Navy to maintain the stranglehold of naval and economic blockade; because mastery of the sea enabled it to transport and sustain Wellington's army in Spain; because Napoleon's rule with its attendant economic shortages became intolerable in Europe, Trafalgar and the continuing blockade of the French coast were the key causes of the Emperor's downfall. An American naval historian, Admiral Mahan, has put it in words which have become famous: "It was those far distant, storm-beaten ships, upon which the Grand Army never looked, which stood between it and the dominion of the world."

right: H.M.S. Victory *at Portsmouth today*

below: H.M.S. Victory *at Gibraltar after the battle*

CHAPTER 10

ANGLO-AMERICAN DUELS

An American was once heard upbraiding an Englishman for his ignorance of the war of 1812-14. Didn't he know that the British burned Washington? "Good heavens!" was the reply, "Did we really? I knew we burned Joan of Arc."

The war figures more largely in American history books because of the striking victories in frigate actions which heralded the birth of the U.S. Navy. To the British it was an annoying and somewhat discreditable episode in the mortal combat with Napoleonic France. With her huge fleets blockading the continent, her frigates chasing French shipping off the seas, and her army fighting under Wellington in Spain, it was not until Napoleon was defeated that she could afford to turn her attention to the other side of the Atlantic.

It was an unnecessary war between cousins, if not brothers, and it did not settle any of the points at issue. American ships fought under two flags: the Stars and Stripes, and a white flag with "FREE TRADE AND SAILORS' RIGHTS" emblazoned on it in red letters. This flag gives some idea of what the war was all about, though in western states the idea of invading Canada was more important. Ever since Trafalgar, Britannia had "ruled the waves"; but Napoleon ruled Europe. When,

H.M.S. Shannon *v*
U.S. frigate
Chesapeake

in the classic struggle between land and sea power, it was found that neutral Americans were delivering contraband cargoes to the enemy, Britain insisted on the right to search such ships. Naturally, the Americans objected and demanded Free Trade.

Right of search?

The demand for Sailors' Rights arose from another wartime grievance. The war with France had gone on so long that thousands of British seamen deserted from the Royal Navy every year. They were attracted by higher wages, quicker promotion, and the hope that they would find life easier on board U.S. warships. In this they were disappointed, because there the lash was used just as frequently as in British ships.

Desertion became such a drain on Britain's limited man-power that she insisted on the right to search foreign ships for deserters. That right was often exercised in a very high-handed way. Moreover, as the Royal Navy grew larger and its press-gangs found it harder to recruit men, many sailors speaking the same language as the Americans, bought forged American passports. It became increasingly difficult to say who was a genuine American, many of whom also found employment on board British ships. Nine such men served on board *H.M.S. Victory* at Trafalgar, and by 1812 there were at least 3,000 serving either voluntarily or by compulsion. Sometimes their consuls obtained their release, if they desired it, but the Admiralty would not let them go without strict enquiries. What could be done about a fellow calling himself Oliver Cromwell whose citizenship papers were dated at New York when he was actually at Plymouth? Every British line-of-battle ship carried a dozen or so Americans; every American frigate carried a few English deserters.

Just at the moment when the British government was prepared to compromise over the Right of Search, President Madison declared war. A week earlier the objectionable Order in Council had been revoked, but the news did not reach the president in time, so slow were transatlantic communications in those days.

The American frigates

The British underestimated the efficiency of the small U.S. Navy because they did not know anything about it. On paper it only amounted to seven frigates and eight sloops. What was not known was that three of these frigates— *United States, President, Constitution*—were really pocket battleships of upwards of fifty guns, whereas frigates normally mounted thirty-six or twenty-four. Nor could the fighting calibre of men like John Rodgers or Isaac Hull be measured as yet.

As soon as war was declared in June, 1812, the offensive-minded Rodgers took three frigates and two sloops to prey upon the vulnerable convoys of British merchantmen returning from the West Indies. He encountered a small frigate, the *Belvidere,* before her captain knew that there was a war on. She escaped because a bow gun on board the *President* exploded, wounding Rodgers in the leg. Running north, the *Belvidere* joined Broke's squadron of frigates stationed at Halifax.

Like Rodgers, Philip Broke was a pugnacious officer dedicated to the naval service. Like him, he was a gunnery enthusiast and alone of

U.S. frigate Constitution

his squadron, his frigate, the *Shannon*, was in a high state of readiness. Her crew had been trained in rapid and accurate fire at a date when most captains scarcely bothered about such things because they were meeting with so little opposition at sea. In the frigate duels which followed they eventually discovered their mistake. However it must be remembered that in every case it was the heavier gunned ship that won, for such is the nature of war.

Broke led his squadron south to New York hoping to encounter Rodgers, but by that time the latter was half way across the Atlantic. On his way, Broke met a little merchant brig. "Well, captain, I must burn your ship," he said. "Burn her? She is all I have in the world. Is it war then?" "Yes," replied Broke, "and I have orders to burn, sink or destroy all enemy shipping." He put his arm round the skipper's shoulders in sympathy. War might be war, but there was also the brotherhood of the sea, and one of the most pleasing aspects of this war at sea was the chivalrous way it was fought on both sides.

Instead of Rodgers, Broke found Isaac Hull in the *Constitution*. The latter was almost cut off by the British *Guerrière,* an old French prize, but she escaped because she was the faster sailer.

A month later, the two ships met again and the superiority of the American frigates was triumphantly demonstrated in the first duel of the war. The *Constitution* had the advantage in weight of metal, tonnage and men; moreover, being just out of port, she was a fast sailer. Captain Dacres fought the old *Guerrière* till she sank, but he was the first British officer to surrender his sword.

H.M.S. Java *dismasted by U.S. frigate* Constitution

A matter of discipline

The same thing happened when the *United States* (Commodore Stephen Decatur) met the *Macedonian* (Captain John Carden) near the Canary Islands on October 25th. Carden had not heard of the loss of the *Guerrière,* but having met Decatur in peace-time at Philadelphia he ought to have known how powerful Decatur's ship was—478 men, compared with his own 290. He had not been in command of the *Macedonian* for long, nor was he a popular captain. A loblolly boy, or surgeon's assistant, named Samuel Leech, who had hoped that he would have been a softer-hearted captain than the last, found he was "like all the others, the same unfeeling, heartless lover of whip discipline."

Leech's words may be taken with a grain of salt, because he wrote his memoirs forty years after the event, as an American citizen. He was the son of a gardener at Blenheim, the home of the Churchills, who volunteered to go to sea at the age of twelve. He found life on board the *Macedonian* not at all what he expected. Official floggings, such as when a man received four dozen lashes from a cat-o'-nine-tails, sickened him. He often heard men say that had it not been fear of what happened to the mutineers of the *Bounty,* they would seize the ship. "I have heard them swear that if ever there was a battle they would shoot their officers." There were a dozen Americans on board against their will. Is it surprising that in this untrained, unhappy ship some of the guns were not properly loaded, or were deliberately misaimed?

It was far otherwise with Decatur. He had commanded the *United States* for the past four years. He had a fine record (and a foul

Commander Stephen Decatur

temper) and his ship was the most powerful in the U.S. Navy. He could afford to allow his opponent to make all the mistakes before he closed in to demolish her.

An overwhelming victory

As soon as there was a cry of "Sail ho!" from the mast-head of the *Macedonian,* Carden ran on deck. "A square-rigged vessel, sir. A large ship standing towards us." If she was a Yankee frigate, what was she doing so far away from the American coast? "All hands clear ship for action!" Drums and fifes beat to quarters as bulkheads were knocked down and the guns run out of the ports. One of the American seamen ran up to the captain asking to be excused from fighting against his fellow countrymen. Carden picked

Capture of H.M.S. Macedonian *by* United States

up a pistol and told the man to go to his post if he didn't want to be shot. He was later killed, says Leech, whose duty, as a boy, was to carry up cartridges to the guns; according to him, every man fought like a tiger when action was joined.

Carden's lieutenant advised his captain to stand across the American's bows to force her to close action. But the captain chose to haul before the wind in order to come up on her from astern. The consequence was that Decatur could open the two-hour action with his longer-range guns while Carden's shot fell far short. As the two ships closed on a parallel course, with the *Macedonian* slightly astern, Leech could feel the ship shudder as she was struck by broadsides from the *United States*. There was a noise like

the tearing of silk, as the shot winged over the deck. It was like being in the middle of a thunderstorm, with lightning flashing from the American's guns. Soon the frigate's decks were covered with blood. Over a hundred men lay dead (the *United States* lost twelve). Carden tried to ram the enemy when his ship could not stand any more heavy fire, but she had lost most of her masts and would not answer her helm. She lay a complete wreck, wallowing between the waves, waiting for the final blow.

Decatur turned away to repair his rigging. An hour later he steered towards the wreck. As he approached, Carden ordered the colours to be struck and rowed across to the *United States*. Looking like a farmer in a plain suit and a straw hat, Decatur received him at the entry port. "I am an undone man," protested Carden, "because I am the first British officer that has struck his flag to an American." "You are mistaken, sir," replied Decatur, "Your *Guerrière* has been taken by us." As Carden proffered his sword, hilt foremost, Decatur added, "I cannot receive the sword of a man who has so bravely defended his ship. But I will receive your hand." And he took him down to his cabin for refreshment.

Kindred spirits

About half the survivors of the *Macedonian* were taken on board the *United States* as prisoners, among them Leech: "I soon felt myself perfectly at home with the American seamen and chose to mess with them. All idea that we had been trying to shoot each other's brains out so shortly before seemed forgotten. We ate together, drank together, joked, laughed, told yarns; in short, a perfect unity of ideas, feelings and purposes seemed to exist among all hands. A corresponding degree of unity, I am told, exists among the officers." Some recognized old shipmates among the American crew; one man met his brother. Is it surprising that Leech accepted an invitation to join the U.S. Navy?

But fate was soon to catch up with him. He found life on board an American ship just as hard as on board an English one. Moreover, the brig he was in was captured and he stood in danger of being hanged as a traitor. The peace treaty saved his neck. He became an American citizen and a respected member of a New England township. To his dying day, he could not forget the cheering crowds at Newport when the *Macedonian* was brought in

with the Stars and Stripes hanging above the British ensign—the first visible token of the superiority of the famous American frigates.

Their triumph did not last long. The British blockade was tightening along the coast, though the *Chesapeake* slipped into Boston after an unsuccessful cruise. She found no money available for wages and many of her ship's company deserted. Her unpopular captain was replaced by Captain James Lawrence—"Captain Jim"— the toast of the town after his eighteen-gun sloop *Hornet* had sunk the *Peacock*. He had not been in command a week before he received orders to go to sea to attack a British convoy.

A chivalrous challenge

But within sight of Boston lighthouse *H.M.S. Shannon* beat up and down on guard. Captain Broke was becoming bored with this sort of duty; he was spoiling for a fight to redeem the honour of the British flag. On 13th May, 1813, only eleven days after Lawrence had been appointed to the command of the *Chesapeake*, Broke sent him a challenge to come out and fight. Lawrence never received it, because he sailed before it could be delivered. Its wording is typical of the way this war was fought. As the *Chesapeake* appeared to be ready for sea (wrote Broke), and as the *Shannon* must soon return to Halifax to replenish her water supply, he asked Lawrence to give him the opportunity "to try the fortune of our respective flags. To an officer of your character, it requires some apology to proceed to further particulars." But he offered to send away any other British ships in the offing if a single ship combat could be arranged between Cape Cod and

Cape Anne. "I doubt not that you, equally confident of success, will feel that it is only by repeated triumphs, in even combats, that your little navy can now hope to console your country for the loss of that trade it can no longer protect."

Lawrence would have agreed. For once, the combat was between equally matched frigates and he had no doubt that a sixth victory would be won in the series of single ship duels.

The *Chesapeake* left Boston on the morning of June 1st. The *Shannon* led her to the appointed duelling ground fifteen miles away. In Lawrence's last letter he said: "I am in hopes to give a good account of her before night. My crew appear to be in fine spirits, and I trust will do their duty."

At four o'clock in the afternoon, when the *Chesapeake* was four miles away and coming up fast,

Broke assembled his men to address them through his speaking trumpet: "Shannons, the time has come to show the superiority you have acquired in managing your guns and in marksmanship. You know the Americans have lately triumphed on several occasions over the British flag. But this will not daunt you. We all know 'twas disparity of force that enabled them to do so. You know the day—'tis the Glorious First of June (referring to Howe's victory in 1794). I have great hopes of adding another shining laurel to it, for I have no doubt we will triumph. Remember your comrades from the *Guerrière,* the *Macedonian,* the *Java.* You have the blood of hundreds to avenge this day. Now go quietly to your quarters and don't cheer."

"Don't give up the ship!"

The two slim frigates manœuvred as if in a yacht race. When about forty yards apart, the crew of the *Chesapeake* roared out their cheers, but those on board the *Shannon* kept silent. The American ranged up alongside. Broke waited until she was almost touching before giving her a devastating broadside with double-shotted guns. The *Chesapeake's* side was smashed in and flying splinters, together with grape-shot from the carronades, struck down almost everyone on deck. Lawrence himself was wounded by a musket ball.

There was so much smoke that no one could tell what was happening. All they could feel was a jar as the two ships fell foul of each other, their yards entangled in deadly embrace. Within a moment, English sailors were running across them to fire down on the deck of the American. Lawrence was hit a

Captain James Lawrence

second time in the groin. As he was taken below he cried, "Don't give up the ship! Tell the men to fire faster. Doctor," he added, as he was laid on the operating table, "go on deck and tell the commanding officer to fight the ship till she sinks."

It was too late. "Captain Broke," shouted a man standing beside him, peering through the smoke, "now is the time to board her, for there's no man alive on her quarterdeck." Dropping his speaking trumpet and snatching up a sword, Broke, in the black top hat he was wearing, scrambled up the stern gallery shouting, "Follow me who can!"

Waves of yelling seamen with cutlasses, pikes and hatchets, surged after him, while the marines kept up a steady covering fire. Some sixty men got on board the *Chesapeake* before the two ships swung apart. They were soon in possession of the upper deck, forcing the Americans down the hatches. Just as the colours were struck down, two Americans attacked Broke, using their muskets like clubs. One hit him on the shoulder, knocking off his hat, the other picked up a cutlass and cut him across the skull, so deeply that part of the brain could be seen palpitating. As Broke leant across a gun the man bandaging him encouraged him with the words, "Look there, sir! There goes the old ensign up over the Yankee colours."

Down below, Lawrence was breathing his last. On being told that the ship had been boarded, his last conscious words were: "Then blow up the ship!"

Lieutenant Provo Wallis, who took over the command of the *Shannon* when Broke was wounded, looked at his watch. The action, the most shattering frigate action in

history, had lasted exactly eleven minutes and the casualty rate was the highest yet recorded. The twenty-five year old lieutenant (who lived to be the oldest naval officer on record, dying as Admiral of the Fleet at the age of a hundred and one), took the two ships to Halifax. Broke recovered from his wound, though he never again served at sea. Lawrence was buried at Halifax before his body was taken home in the *United States*.

His cry when he was wounded, "Don't give up the ship!" became part of the folklore of the American people. The first to be inspired by it was Commodore Oliver Hazard Perry, who had a blue flag made with the words sewn onto it in white. He also named his flagship the *Lawrence* to commemorate his old friend.

The Battle of Lake Erie

Perry was in command of the naval forces on Lake Erie. It will be recalled that the conquest of Canada was one of the reasons for the war. The frontier was ill defined and sparsely inhabited. Control of Lakes Champlain, Ontario and Erie was essential, but there were no warships in this part of the world. After British soldiers had captured Detroit and American frontiersmen had burned York (now Toronto), a furious race in shipbuilding commenced. Everything—shipwrights, sailors, guns, tools of all sorts—had to be brought from the east. Strange craft soon appeared on the slips, the largest of about 600 tons, none of them fit to last because they were built in a hurry of unseasoned timber. Within a year, the naval contest on the lakes was more important than military skirmishes on land.

Defending Detroit at the west end of Lake Erie, Captain Robert Barclay, a thirty-two-year old

veteran of Trafalgar, where he had lost an arm, had six ships of all sizes and 440 men at his disposal. His supplies were running out, so he had to challenge the enemy before he could build up a squadron more than two-thirds their size.

At the other end of the lake, Perry had nine ships and 532 men, a motley collection with which he moved up to Put-in-Bay, where the lake narrows on the way to Detroit. He called his flagship the *Lawrence,* intending that she and the *Niagara* should bear the brunt of the battle with Barclay's two largest ships, *Detroit* and *Queen Charlotte.* The rest of the craft on both sides were so small that they did not matter, even though they formed up into line of battle.

Perry had not foreseen the damage which Barclay could do him at long range. He was badly supported by the *Niagara,* which dropped astern, so that within a few minutes his ship was a burning wreck. Leaving the Stars and Stripes still flying, he left the ship, and with four sailors, climbed into a boat towing astern. Clutching the blue flag with Lawrence's words embroidered on it, they rowed across to the *Niagara.* Fortunately for him, Barclay's two ships collided, and they were so fiercely attacked by the smaller craft that they soon surrendered. Perry then rowed back to resume command of his flagship, on which two-thirds of the American casualties had occurred.

His laconic despatch sums up the results of this action on the Great Lakes, the only one to have been fought there. "We have met the enemy and they are ours; two ships, two brigs, one sloop, one schooner." To-day, a monument at the western end of Lake Erie commemorates his refusal to admit defeat in the last American victory of the war.

Heaving the lead

U.S. frigate Constitution *at Malta 1837*

CHAPTER 11

NAVARINO

The last battle under sail was fought on 20th October, 1827, in the bay of Navarino, often called Navarin. In this same wide bay on the southern tip of the Greek coast, an Athenian fleet had forced the Spartans to surrender during the Peloponnesian War in 425 B.C. The place is only a hundred miles or so south of Lepanto, the site of the last battle between galleys, and the enemy in 1827, as in 1571, was the Ottoman fleet, assisted by squadrons from the vassal provinces of Egypt and Tunis.

But whereas Lepanto was the climax of a European crusade against advancing Turks, Navarino was an accidental battle against a declining empire. It was said that the guns of the ships belonging to the great powers almost went off by themselves, because the reactionary governments of western Europe had no desire to see the Ottoman empire broken up by an action which secured the independence of Greece in the name of nationalism. In their eyes this decisive victory on the part of a British-French-Russian fleet was (as the British government described it) "an untoward event", that is to say, an unexpected and somewhat unfortunate victory over "an ancient ally," as the Turkish empire was inaccurately called.

Hence the story of what happened at Navarino is full of irony. No

The Battle of Navarino

Greek was present, except as a spectator, in a battle which secured the independence of Greece as a nation state. The successful commander-in-chief was recalled for exceeding his instructions. All the allied admirals had been told to avoid hostilities, but their orders made such a conflict inevitable. When it was all over, the governments pretended that nothing had happened, whereas in reality a new state had been added to the family of nations.

The Greek cause

European governments at that date were quite out of touch with the liberal opinions held by large sections of the population. When the Greek revolt against their Turkish masters began in 1821 there was a surge of sympathy on the part of the classically educated classes, thousands of whom in every land called themselves "philhellenes." Victor Hugo and Shelley wrote poems in support of the cause; Byron died at Missolonghi in 1824 as an internationally famous martyr to Greek independence. Volunteers like Lord Cochrane (recently returned from liberating Chile, Peru and Brazil from European imperialism), or Colonel Fabvier tried unsuccessfully to organize Greek resistance. It was all of no avail: in June 1827 Athens surrendered after a long siege. Never had the fortunes of Greek patriots stood lower.

The chief reason for Turkish success was the Sultan's reliance on the help of his vassal, Mehemet Ali, a humble Albanian by birth who rose to be Pasha of Egypt and was soon to create an Egyptian state independent of the Ottoman Porte. His thirty-eight-year old son, Ibrahim, was a genius as a soldier,

but he had no experience at sea. Now governor of the Peloponnese (or Morea, as it was then called), he defeated whatever Greek forces appeared in the field and proceeded to lay waste the peninsula and massacre its inhabitants.

It was barbaric behaviour of this sort which compelled the governments of Europe to intervene. The only remaining Greek resistance was on the part of the fishermen-pirates whom Cochrane and Captain Abney Hastings were trying to organize into a navy. Rich Philhellenes promised them the assistance of steam warships which, had they appeared in time, would have been the first steamships in action. Official circles regarded such adventurers as worse than the Turks. The only solution appeared to be the presence of an allied fleet which would prevent Ibrahim and his masters from perpetrating further barbarities.

The Treaty of London

For this purpose, the Treaty of London was signed in July, 1827, between Britain, France and Russia, with the approval of Austria. Orders were sent to the commanders of the respective squadrons in the Mediterranean to unite off southern Greece and maintain a pacific blockade which would cut off Ibrahim's supplies from Alexandria. Never were orders more ambiguous. The admirals were to defend the Greeks, but must not allow their proceedings to "degenerate into hostilities" by fighting their oppressors. No admiral must serve under another, but all must co-operate in preserving "the spirit of the agreement of peaceful interference by a friendly demonstration of force." The British admiral was advised to keep the peace through his speaking trumpet.

Ibrahim-Pasha

The Russian was told privately by the Tsar to destroy the Turks *à la russe*. The Frenchman shrugged his shoulders and told his wife that *toutes ces hostilités sans hostilité sont trop subtiles pour moi*. Since in those days it took a month to receive orders from a European capital, all three were left to take responsibility for anything which might happen. What did happen at Navarino is therefore a remarkable tribute to the fellowship of the sea and the good sense of the admirals involved.

Admiral Codrington

The allied fleet

Sir Edward Codrington was the senior admiral merely because of his experience and the size of his force; his flagship *Asia* being an eighty-four-gun ship. Before taking any action he consulted his colleagues, with whom he was on excellent terms after he had overcome his suspicions of his French colleague, suspicions which were quite natural after a century's warfare between them. He was a forthright, pugnacious character with a fine naval record. At Trafalgar he had commanded a ship with distinction. Since the present action was fought on the eve of the anniversary of that battle, he was tactless enough to remind the French admiral of Nelson's advice on that occasion. It says much for the French admiral that he nobly supported Codrington on the day of battle. There is a story that the Lord High Admiral, the Duke of Clarence (later King William IV), who had been brought up in the navy, was so impatient of the ambiguous instructions sent by his government that he told Codrington "Go in, Ned, and smash those damned Turks." The Tsar certainly used such language, but none of the commanders on the spot wished to exceed their official instructions.

The Comte de Rigny, the French admiral, had been in the eastern Mediterranean longer than either of his colleagues and knew far more about the complicated situation that confronted them. At first Codrington suspected that he was more of a diplomatist than a sailor, but he soon found him a reliable companion in arms. The Russian admiral was easier. "An open-hearted man", said Codrington, "who kept his ships clean and seaworthy"—unusual virtues in a Russian fleet. Possibly this was because Count Heiden was a Dutchman who, after service in the British

Admiral De Rigny

119

navy, had joined the Russian, as so many foreigners did at that time.

On the day of battle, Codrington, De Rigny and Heiden had at their disposal twenty-four ships, of which eleven were ships of the line. It is impossible to enumerate Ibrahim's fleet because so many of his vessels were transports, fire-ships and small craft, but the allies reckoned that he had at least sixty-five warships, of which three were line-of-battle ships (on board them were at least six Frenchmen as volunteer officers) and twenty frigates, all under the command of Moharren Bey, Ibrahim's brother-in-law, when the latter was absent with the army.

Diplomatic exchange

Codrington was the first of the allies to arrive in the area on September 12th, soon to be joined by De Rigny. They arranged an interview with Ibrahim in his tent outside the walls of the citadel of Navarino. Over Turkish coffee, served in tiny silver cups, and puffs at a pipe of peace encrusted with jewels, it was agreed that an armistice would be preserved. Both sides realized that this was merely papering over the cracks, because Cochrane and Hastings were fighting for the liberation of Greece in the Gulf of Patras, less than a hundred miles away, and Ibrahim was straining at the leash to suppress them. His troops were laying waste the Morea and such pirates (as he called them) were not to be tolerated. Codrington sent urgent messages to restrain them, but they took no notice. At one point Ibrahim actually took his fleet to sea, but then thought better of it and returned to Navarino. One more incident, followed by reprisals, would be the end of the armistice.

On October 17th, the allied fleet was finally united by the arrival of

the Russian squadron, with Heiden in the *Azov* as his flagship. The same day there arrived yet more news of another massacre on the mainland. Codrington therefore sent the *Dartmouth* frigate into the bay with a protest signed by all the admirals. But Ibrahim had left for the interior and no contact could be made with him. He did not return until the day after the battle in which his fleet was destroyed.

Broken armistice

On October 20th, the allies decided to enter the bay as a demonstration of force rather than with any inten-

The Allied fleet
entering Navarino Bay

tion of fighting. When the governor of the citadel saw what they intended he refused them the right of entry, threatening to fire on the ships as they passed under his guns. Codrington replied that he was not there to receive orders but to give them. With the *Asia* leading and bands playing, the fleet slowly entered the bay in which a multitude of Egyptian shipping lay at anchor in a vast horseshoe formation.

Whatever the intentions of the high command, the crews of every ship were prepared for action. An account written by a boy seaman on board H.M.S. *Genoa,* Charles McPherson by name, describes how

he wrote at the dictation of one of his shipmates a last letter to the man's mother: "Can't say if you'll ever get another letter from me, for we mean to go in tomorrow to Navarino Bay to beat the Turks, so whether I'll be sent to Davy (i.e. drowned) or not I cannot tell; but you must not fret, dear mother, if I should be called away tomorrow, for you know that death is a debt we must pay." The man was killed next day and young McPherson pushed the body overboard after reading the funeral service himself because the chaplain was too busy elsewhere.

He tells how the gun crew of which he was a member, were

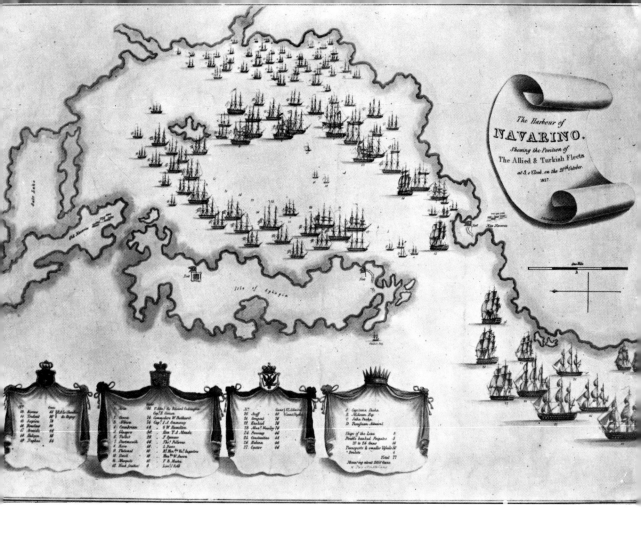

The harbour of Navarino, showing the position of the Allied and Turkish fleets, from a contemporary print

ordered to double shot their guns as they entered the bay. The lieutenant in charge was the son of Captain Broke of *Shannon* fame: "Now, my men, you see we are going into harbour today. I know that you'll be right glad of it; at least, I suppose you would be as much against cruising off here all winter as I am. So, I say, let's fight it out like British seamen, and if we fall, why there's an end of our cruise." As the drums beat to quarters, much the same speech with the same preparation for action-stations was made on board every allied ship.

Seeing that the biggest enemy ships were lying in the centre of the horseshoe, Codrington and De Rigny steered directly towards them, directing Heiden to look after the Egyptian right wing. The guns of the batteries at the entrance of the bay could have stopped them, but a French officer describes how he saw the Turkish gunners peacefully smoking their pipes on the battlements. By half past two in the afternoon the allied ships anchored alongside the enemy, the general orders having been carried out that "no gun is to be fired from the combined fleet without a signal being made for that purpose, unless shot be fired from any of the Turkish ships; in which case the ship so firing is to be destroyed immediately. In case of a regular battle ensuing and creating any of that confusion which naturally arises from it, it is to be observed that, in the words of Lord Nelson, 'No captain can do very wrong who places his ship alongside that of an enemy.' ''

Captain Fellowes of the *Dartmouth* was told to watch the fire-ships placed at the end of the enemy line, because if they were loosed, indescribable havoc could be caused among the 150 ships huddled together in the bay. If ever there was an explosive situation, it was this. The orders on board the ships on both sides rang out: "Stand to your guns!" and the replies could be heard in the calm of the afternoon: "All ready, sir!" Seeing some movement among the fire-ships, Fellowes sent a boat to tell them not to move. "Recollect, sir," he told the lieutenant in charge, "that no act of hostility is to be attempted by us on any account."

The Battle of Navarino

As the boat drew near the fire-ship, a shot rang out and the coxswain

dropped dead. Other shots followed and the Turks could be seen igniting the train of gunpowder on board. Another boat was hastily despatched, but the lieutenant was shot dead as the ship caught alight.

The height of the battle

The end of the battle

De Rigny, having seen what happened from the quarterdeck of the *Sirène,* shouted through his speaking trumpet to the captain of the Egyptian ship near him that he would not fire first. The reply was a broadside. He immediately gave the order to fire and, as he remarked, the action became general.

It is impossible to describe the turmoil of the next three hours. Anchored alongside each other, there was no question of man-œuvring. Rival ships battered each other at the closest range. As soon as the French flagship opened fire, Codrington sent an interpreter to Moharren Bey to tell him he would not fire first. The man was shot with a pistol as he came up the side. The *Asia* opened fire and within twenty minutes the Egyptian flagship was a flaming wreck.

On board the *Genoa,* Lieutenant Broke "gave the word, FIRE! and immediately the whole tier of guns was discharged with terrific effect into the side of the Turkish admiral's ship that lay abreast of us. After this it was 'Fire away, my boys, as hard as you can!' The first man I saw killed in our ship (continues McPherson) was a marine. He was close beside me. Turning round, I saw him at my feet with his head fairly severed from his body, as if it had been done with a knife. The firing continued incessant, accompanied occasionally by loud cheers, which were not drowned even in the roar of artillery; but distincter than these could be heard the dismal shrieks of the sufferers, that sounded like death knells in the ear."

The bombardment continued until darkness fell about six o'clock. The scale of gunfire can be calculated from the figures for the amount of shot expended by the three largest English ships: *Asia*—forty tons, *Albion*—fifty tons, *Genoa*—thirty

tons. According to a French officer, the only enemy ships left afloat the next morning were a dismasted frigate, four corvettes and ten brigs. It was estimated that over a thousand of the enemy were killed and three thousand wounded. On the allied side the British lost seventy-five killed, the French forty-three and the Russians fifty-nine.

Codrington told his wife: "Now, my dear, don't fancy anything more than I tell you. I am entirely unhurt, but the *Asia* is quite a wreck, having had her full allowance of the work.

Turkish flagship blowing up

Our men fired beautifully; my two colleagues and the brave men they commanded behaved admirably; and nothing could exceed the style in which my own ships went into action."

De Rigny, in a letter written the same day, said that the plan he had proposed was a complete success. Certainly that was true of the battle, but no action was less planned beforehand. By cutting off Ibrahim's supplies, the victory at Navarino secured the independence of Greece, which was formally acknowledged two years later by the Treaty of Adrianople.

Sea power had achieved what Ibrahim's success on land could not win. When, ten years later, he and his father tried to destroy the remnants of the Ottoman empire in the interests of Egyptian independence, they were checked once more by sea power at Acre. But on that occasion it was sea power in the form of steamships.

The battle of Navarino marked the end of the era of sea fights under sail.

ACKNOWLEDGEMENTS

The author and Publishers make grateful acknowledgement to the following for permission to reproduce copyright illustrations. Cover and endpaper illustrations from National Maritime Museum. British Museum: pp. 32 (top), 35 (bottom right), 58 (top left). Mansell Collection: p. 17 (top & bottom). Musée de la Marine, Paris: pp. 47, 48, 51, 52 (bottom left), 71 (top), 78, 118, 119 (bottom). National Maritime Museum: pp. 6 & 7, 8, 9, 10,11 (top, centre, bottom), 13, 14 & 15, 16, 18, 23, 24 & 25, 26 (top & bottom), 27, 29, 30, 31, 32 (bottom), 33 (top & bottom), 34 & 35, 36 & 37, 38 (top left, bottom right), 39 (top, bottom right), 40 & 41, 41, 42, 43, 44 (bottom), 45, 46, 53, 54 & 55, 56, 56 & 57, 58 (bottom left, top right), 59, 61, 62, 63 (bottom), 64 & 65, 66, 67, 68, 69 (bottom), 70, 71 (bottom), 72, 73, 75, 76 & 77, 81, 83, 85, 86, 88 & 89, 90, 91, 92, 93, 94, 96, 97, 99, 100, 101, 102, 103, 104 & 105, 108, 110, 113, 114, 115 (top), 116 & 117, 119 (top), 120 & 121, 122, 123, 124 & 125, 126. National Portrait Gallery: p. 82. Rijksmuseum, Amsterdam: p. 44 (top). SCALA, Florence: pp. 20 & 21. Science Museum: pp. 49, 52 (bottom right), 63 (top), 79. Sjöhistoriska Museum, Stockholm: p. 12. U.S. Naval Academy Museum, Annapolis: pp. 69 (top), 107, 109, 112, 115.
Mrs. Tucker of the National Maritime Museum for her invaluable assistance.
Battle plans designed by John C. Gardner, D.A., M.S.I.A.

BIBLIOGRAPHY

Anderson, R. C. 1947. *The Sailing Ship*. Harrap, London.
Gibson, C. E. 1958. *The Story of the Ship*. Abelard-Schuman, London.
Gladstone, E. W. 1958. *The Royal Navy*. Blackwell, Oxford.
Hale, J. R. 1931. *Famous Sea Fights*. Methuen, London.
Lancaster, B. 1958. *The American Revolution*. American Heritage.
Marx, H. F. 1966. *Battle of Lepanto*. World Publishing Company, Cleveland, Ohio.
Mordal, J. 1959. *Twenty-five Centuries of Sea Warfare*. Souvenir Press, London.
Uden, Grant. 1965. *The Fighting Temeraire*. Batsford, London.
Warner, Oliver. 1963. *Great Sea Battles*. Weidenfeld and Nicolson, London.
Warner, Oliver. 1958. *Nelson and the Age of Fighting Sail*. American Heritage.
Warner, Oliver. 1965. *Nelson's Battles*. Batsford, London.
Warner, Oliver. 1958. *The Sea and the Sailors' World*. American Heritage.
Welch, I. 1964. *Famous Sea Battles*. Arthur Barker, London.
Wilcox, L. A. 1966. *Mr. Pepys' Navy*. Bell, London.